Millie

THE COLLECTOR'S ENCYCLOPEDIA OF
OCCUPIED JAPAN

COLLECTIBLES
5TH SERIES

GENE FLORENCE

COLLECTOR BOOKS

A Division of Schroeder Publishing Co., Inc.

Searching For A Publisher?

We are always looking for knowledgeable people considered to be experts within their fields. If you feel that there is a real need for a book on your collectible subject and have a large comprehensive collection, contact us.

COLLECTOR BOOKS
P.O. Box 3009
Paducah, Kentucky 42002-3009

Additional copies of this book may be ordered from:

COLLECTOR BOOKS
P.O. Box 3009
Paducah, KY 42002-3009

or

Gene Florence
(May 1–Oct. 31)	(Nov. 1–April 30)
P.O. Box 22186	P.O. Box 64
Lexington, KY 40522	Astatula, FL 34705

@$14.95. Add $2.00 for postage and handling.

Copyright: Gene Florence, 1992
Values Updated 1994

Printed by IMAGE GRAPHICS, INC., Paducah, Kentucky

FOREWORD

"Made in Occupied Japan" has been a magic phrase to some collectors for years, but as many new collectors join the fraternity, the supply of pieces marked with those magic words decreases daily. In the two years since my **Fourth** book, there have been several newspaper articles carried nationally about this collecting arena. Although there was misinformation and a lack of vital information on several fields within this collectible, it has given an awareness of the words *Occupied Japan* to many people who had no idea that there were collectors looking for items marked in this way.

For those readers who have not seen the previous editions, I will reiterate some basic information.

All items made in Japan (from the beginning of our occupation at the end of World War II until April 28, 1952, when the occupation ended), that were to be exported to the United States had to be marked in one of four ways: "Japan," "Made in Occupied Japan," "Occupied Japan," or "Made in Japan." You can see that if all the markings were used equally or nearly so, still only about half of the items imported into the United States would have been marked with the magic words for collectors, "Made in OCCUPIED JAPAN." Thus, too, you will find that there are many similar or like items which you will find marked only "Japan" or "Made in Japan." There is no way of proving these were actually made in Occupied Japan. (For the sake of brevity, capital letters "MIOJ" and "OJ" will be used throughout the remainder of this book to mean "Made in Occupied Japan" or "Occupied Japan.") I must emphasize that unless an item actually says *occupied* in some form, it cannot be considered to be such. The only exception to that rule would apply to items found in original containers such as boxes or cartons where the container is marked "MIOJ" while the items within are only marked "Japan." These items must always stay with the original container to be collected as *occupied*. From past observation and correspondence with collectors over the years, it is obvious that a large number of items imported from Japan during this time were marked on the containers only and, of course, many of these original containers have been discarded. The items were marked to satisfy governmental policies. The original consumers did not care whether an item was marked "OJ" or not. It is speculated that only a small percentage of the larger, finer wares were themselves marked "MIOJ." The dearth of these larger marked pieces today makes them avidly sought by collectors and very desirable to own. If you have a choice between buying one quality piece or several smaller items, I recommend you consider buying the one.

All items in this book are marked OJ or MIOJ in some form unless noted. If it is not marked Occupied Japan in some form, then there is *no way* to prove that it is! Many times only the box or one item in a set will be marked. In the case of salt and pepper sets, the shakers will be sitting on something marked MIOJ , but the shakers themselves may not be marked MIOJ.

If no color is listed for an item, then the mark is black. All other colors and markings will be listed in parentheses. Measurements to the nearest eighth of an inch are given for several pieces on each page, and if needed, additional measurements have been added. This should help you in pricing similar pieces of OJ. There are many pieces of Occupied Japan that can be found in several sizes. In most cases, bigger is better; however, quality of the item is a major determining factor also!

Be aware that there are counterfeits available and you can read about these in my **Third** book. If the item is glazed on the bottom, the mark will be under the glaze and not on top of it! After a while, experience will enable you to spot an Occupied Japan piece before you even turn it over to look for the mark.

There is an Occupied Japan Collectors Club on the East coast which has an annual show! You can get additional information by sending a SASE to: O.J. Club c/o Florence Archambalt, 29 Freeborn Street, Dept GF, Newport, RI 02840. Dues are $15.00 yearly and there is a monthly newsletter.

ACKNOWLEDGEMENTS

As with my **Fourth** book a special thanks to my family for pitching in and helping make this book possible. It all started with Marc, my son, and Cathy going to Wisconsin to pick up a 10,000 piece collection of Occupied Japan a few years ago when I had my arm in a sling with a broken wrist. Cathy and Marc had to do the wrapping, packing and loading since I was only a supervisor. Marc still believes today that Dad is crazy for being in this business especially when all that "stuff" would not fit in my van and a second trip to pick up the rest had to be made two months later!

Grannie Bear, Cathy, Sibyl and I then spent a week at home unwrapping, sorting and packing this collection and (all the other MIOJ I had purchased over the last two years) for the photography session. We photographed for two books at one time. All of the photographs for the **Fourth** book and most of this **Fifth** book were done in one week long session. Assembling categories together and eliminating items previously shown in the earlier books was a gigantic six day, dawn to midnight, undertaking!

The photography for the book was done by Tom Clouser of Curtis and Mays in Paducah, Kentucky. At the studio we were aptly aided in arranging this into some further semblance of order by Steve Quertermous, Jane White and Teri Hatch. (I hope this Occupied Japan marathon session was not one of the determining factors which caused each of our helpers to leave Collector Books since then.) Cathy had more "thrills" than she wanted in unwrapping, recording the markings and measuring the pieces in each photograph before wrapping them again. We hope you will enjoy all our efforts to show you this little peek at our "Occupied Japan World."

PRICING

All prices in this book are retail. The last thing I do for any book is to go over the prices, updating any new developments that may occur after the writing is finished. This is not as critical in "OJ" as in other fields of collecting, but with publishing lead times as they are today, I want you to know that the prices are current. I sell hundreds of pieces of "MIOJ" in my shop each year with one sale in excess of seven thousand dollars. I only mention this to let you know that the prices listed are not "hoped-for" prices, but actual selling prices. Many of the items shown will now be for sale in my shop; and by the time you read this, most of the best items will already have new homes. I try to spread the sale of the better pieces over a period of time, but if someone says, "I will take them all," then they own them!

You will see higher prices for "OJ" than are listed in this book. I say that for the lady in California who lectured me at length that I priced OJ way too cheaply. I am aware that you will find a few pieces cheaper than those listed. I say that for the man in Pennsylvania, who wrote the same week the lady called, to say I priced OJ so high that nobody in the world could get those prices out of it. Yard and garage sales as well as auctions are good sources for finding bargains on "OJ," but more and more people are becoming aware of those magic words "MIOJ." Be prepared to pay a fair price and hope to find a bargain or two. You will see the same overpriced items time and time again in your travels. Remember that someday you may find the same item at an affordable price. If not, you can chuckle to yourself, as I do, over the prices you see the item not selling for again at shows or in a shop. Unfortunately, people with a little bit of knowledge about "MIOJ" sometimes think that they have a gold mine if they own it.

This book is meant as a guide only. The buyer and the seller determine actual worth. If a mutually agreeable price can be arranged between these two, then that is the price no matter what the book says! I buy and sell. I have to make those decisions often. Many times I leave pieces I would love to have but believe the price is out of line. You have to determine your limits as a collector. I repeat, these prices are meant to be a good, general guide.

Prices are listed as retail; thus, if you want to sell some of your collection to a dealer, you will have to discount them. Most dealers are willing to pay 50% to 60% of the retail price of most items. Common pieces or hard to sell items will be discounted more. Remember the better the piece or the more unusual it is, the more collectors will be looking for it.

Collectors are looking for mint items. The prices listed in this book are for mint condition items. That means having all the parts; no cracks, chips or glued pieces are acceptable. Unless it is very unusual and hard to get, there is little value to damaged pieces.

As in the previous books, I have included a price range for each piece. Several collectors have told me, "I buy at low book and sell at high." Be your own judge. It is your money and only you determine how you spend it — unless you are married, that is!

TABLE OF CONTENTS

ANGELS and CHERUBS

As we begin this fifth pilgrimage into "Occupied Japan" collecting, I would like to reiterate (for those of you who don't read introductions), that if no color is listed for the mark **"OCCUPIED JAPAN"**, then the marking is in **BLACK**. All pieces shown are marked with the word **"OCCU-PIED"** in some form. That word may, oft times, be misspelled; but each piece has to be marked **"OCCUPIED"** for it to be considered a collectible of this genre. Some newcomers to the collecting of "Occupied Japan" want to include unmarked items, but it is **only** the **mark** of **"OCCUPIED JAPAN"** that sets the parameters of this collecting field to those years of the occupation!

Most pieces are listed by size (as they were in the last book). In rows where all pieces are much the same height, the first piece in the row is sized for reference. I received many letters asking me to continue that practice.

As a matter of reference, in this picture, angels are winged and cherubs are not winged.

Most of the finer pieces shown herein are also identified as a product of "Andrea," "Ucagco" or "Ardalt." This holds true for the majority of quality bisque figures marked "Occupied Japan."

Top Row:
1st, Cherub, 5¾", "Ucagco China" w/emblem (gold)	$25.00 – 30.00
2nd and 5th, Cherubs, marked as above	30.00 – 35.00 ea.
3rd and 4th, Angels playing tambourine, 7¼" "Ucagco China" w/emblem	60.00 – 75.00 ea.

Second Row:
1st, Angel on pink basket, 5" (red)	40.00 – 45.00
2nd, Angel with shell on back, 5⅛" (red)	40.00 – 45.00
3rd, Angel sitting on cornucopia (red H.P. Andrea)	50.00 – 55.00
4th, Angel w/donkey, 4⅛" (red)	25.00 – 30.00

Third Row:
1st, Cherub holding bowl, 5½" (red)	40.00 – 45.00
2nd, Angel fixing halo (red)	35.00 – 45.00
3rd, Angel at anvil (red)	35.00 – 40.00
4th, Angel w/donkey (Ardalt 5296 w/**AA** crossed emblem)	50.00 – 60.00

Fourth Row:
1st, Cherub vase, 3⅜" (red)	12.50 – 15.00
2nd, Angel w/shell (red)	30.00 – 35.00
3rd, Angel w/wheelbarrow (red)	25.00 – 30.00
4th and 5th Angel bud vases, 5¼" (red)	15.00 – 17.50 ea.

Fifth Row:
1st, Angel planter (H.P. Andrea)	30.00 – 35.00
2nd and 4th, Angels on butterfly (red)	17.50 – 20.00 ea.
3rd, Powder box ("Ucagco China" w/emblem, gold)	75.00 – 90.00
5th, Angel w/shell (red)	25.00 – 30.00

ANIMALS and BIRDS

These figures run the gamut from cheaply made to highly detailed creations – the difference between department store items and those mass produced for the five and dime stores.

Top Row:

1st, Plume tail peacock, 5"	$17.50 – 20.00
2nd, Flamingo "Lefton China"	20.00 – 22.50
3rd, Bird (red)	2.50 – 4.00
4th, Blue birds (red handwritten Occupied Japan)	7.50 – 10.00
5th, Small birds on limb	2.00 – 3.00
6th, Bird w/long tail (red)	4.00 – 5.00
7th, Penguin (red)	6.00 – 7.00
8th, Fancy plume tailed peacock	15.00 – 17.50

Second Row:

1st and 2nd, Birds on limb	2.00 – 3.00 ea.
3rd, Duck w/hat	6.00 – 8.00
4th and 6th, Birds on limb (blue)	7.50 – 10.00 ea.
5th, Bird on limb (red)	7.50 – 10.00
7th, Birds on stump	8.00 – 10.00

Third Row:

1st and 3rd, Chick	2.00 – 3.00 ea.
2nd, Swan	2.50 – 4.00
4th and 8th – 11th Birds (red)	2.50 – 4.00 ea.
5th – 7th, Birds	2.50 – 4.00 ea.

Fourth Row:

1st, Frog w/accordion (blue)	10.00 – 12.50
2nd, Frog w/bass fiddle	10.00 – 12.50
3rd, Frog on lily pad (red circle **T**)	17.50 – 20.00
4th, Frog drummer (red)	17.50 – 20.00
5th, Frog w/accordion (blue)	17.50 – 20.00
6th and 7th, Frog w/violin or mandolin (red)	15.00 – 17.50 ea.

Fifth Row:

1st, Bear w/hat	8.00 – 10.00
2nd, Hugging pandas (red)	10.00 – 12.50
3rd, Brown bear (blue circle **T**)	10.00 – 12.50
4th, Polar bear (?) (red)	5.00 – 6.00
5th, Frog ash tray (red)	10.00 – 12.50
6th, Frog vase (red)	12.50 – 15.00
7th, Bisque frog fish bowl ornament	10.00 – 12.50
8th, Reclining frog, (red circle **T**)	15.00 – 17.50

ANIMALS – CATS AND DOGS

Cats and dogs are the animals most often sought by collectors. I have sold more of these figures to people who were not concerned that they were marked Occupied Japan than to many of the collectors of this ware. Admittedly, many of these animals are caricatures, but the quality pieces which look like certain breeds are always the first pieces to sell when I bring collections into my shop.

Siamese cats and poodles seem to be the most in demand, but German shepherds and collies are also in short supply for all the collectors looking for them.

Top Row:

1st, Cat planter, 3⅝" (horseshoe emblem)	$8.00 – 10.00
2nd, Cat sitting (green circle **T**)	20.00 – 22.50
3rd, Cat reclining (green circle **T**)	20.00 – 22.50
4th, Cat planter (arch emblem)	5.00 – 6.00
5th, Cat w/bow	6.00 – 8.00

Second Row:

1st, Cat w/pert expression	2.50 – 4.00
2nd, Cat w/kitten	2.50 – 4.00
3rd, Black cat w/basket (blue)	5.00 – 6.00
4th, Cat w/bee-like tail (red)	2.50 – 4.00
5th, Cat w/bow (red)	4.00 – 5.00
6th, Cat w/paw up (red)	4.00 – 5.00
7th, Cat w/tail up (blue)	5.00 – 6.00
8th, Cat w/tiger tail (red)	2.50 – 4.00
9th, Black cat (embossed)	5.00 – 6.00

Third Row:

1st, Curly tail cat (blue)	2.50 – 4.00
2nd – 4th, Set w/ball, yarn, bug (red)	2.00 – 3.00 ea.
5th and 7th, Cats in potty (blue)	2.00 – 3.00 ea.
6th, Cat w/ red yarn	5.00 – 6.00
8th, Bull dog with rubber tail (red)	7.50 – 10.00
9th, Dog sitting	5.00 – 6.00
10th, Dog walking (red)	2.50 – 4.00

Fourth Row:

1st and 2nd, Yellow and blue dog planters, 4" (Arch emblem)	4.00 – 5.00 ea.
3rd and 4th, Long dogs (# symbol)	6.00 – 8.00
5th, Dog w/hat and pipe, 3½" (red)	10.00 – 12.50
6th, Dog, same except 2⅜"	5.00 – 6.00

Fifth Row:

1st and 2nd, Brown or black dog planters (Arch emblem)	5.00 – 6.00 ea.
3rd, Dog sitting	8.00 – 10.00
4th, Spotted dog planter	5.00 – 6.00
5th and 6th, Dog planters (Arch emblem)	5.00 – 6.00 ea.

ANIMALS and INSECTS

The Japanese, with their appreciation of beauty, often surround themselves with flowers and miniature, ornate gardens. Perhaps those inspired their fascination with lady bugs shown in the bottom three rows on page 11. I originally called these "bees" in some of my earlier books, but it is easy to see upon closer inspection that these are not bees—if you're an entomologist, which I am not.

The jumping horses in the top row are very fine porcelain figures. Quality workmanship in animal figures is hard to find. Most animal figures seem to be symbolic or caricatures.

Top Row:

1st, Pony	$ 6.00 – 8.00
2nd, Jumping horses 5" (blue circle **T**)	35.00 – 45.00
3rd and 4th, Horses (red)	12.50 – 15.00 ea.
5th, Donkey	6.00 – 8.00
6th, Deer (maybe)	2.50 – 4.00

Second Row:

1st, Metal horse w/saddle (embossed)	10.00 – 12.50
2nd, Metal donkey w/prospecting gear (embossed)	10.00 – 12.50
3rd, Saddle horse w/cork (red)	10.00 – 12.00
4th, Deer (green circle **T**)	6.00 – 8.00
5th, Cow (blue)	8.00 – 10.00
6th, Goat (red)	6.00 – 8.00

Third Row:

1st, Lady bug w/bat, 2¼"	6.00 – 8.00
2nd and 3rd, Lady bug w/bowler hat or umbrella	5.00 – 6.00 ea.
4th, Lady bug w/newspaper	5.00 – 6.00
5th, Lady bug w/bass fiddle and top hat, 3"	6.00 – 8.00
6th, Lady bug w/mandolin and polka dot hat	6.00 – 8.00
7th, Lady bug w/ horn and turban	6.00 – 8.00
8th, Lady bug w/violin (blue)	6.00 – 8.00
9th, Lady bug w/bag (red)	5.00 – 6.00
10th, Lady bug w/accordion (red)	6.00 – 8.00

Fourth Row:

1st, Lady bug w/vest 3½" (blue)	7.50 – 10.00
2nd, Lady bug ice man (red #92795)	10.00 – 12.50
3rd, Lady bug w/lantern (red "Ucagco China" w/emblem #927)	10.00 – 12.50
4th and 5th, Lady bug w/soda and singer (blue)	7.50 – 10.00 ea.
6th, Lady bug w/buggy	6.00 – 8.00
7th, Lady bug w/camera	10.00 – 12.50

Fifth Row:

1st, Lady bug w/bat, 4"	12.50 – 15.00
2nd, Lady bug w/broom (brown #92796)	10.00 – 12.50
3rd, Lady bug w/umbrella	10.00 – 12.50
4th, Lady bug Indian w/pipe and heart loin cloth	12.50 – 15.00
5th, Same marked (red #92795)	12.50 – 15.00
6th, Lady bug w/newspaper	10.00 – 12.50
7th, Lady bug hobo	10.00 – 12.50

ASH TRAYS and CIGARETTE BOXES

Accumulating ash trays and cigarette items has lately fallen out of favor in most collecting circles; but there are some fairly fancy ones in Occupied Japan items if you wish to search for them.

The cigarette boxes in the second row have their lids displayed to show the designs. The matching ash trays for these boxes are shown on the third row.

Those cigarette boxes shown in the bottom two rows probably have matching ash trays, but they were not found with the boxes when I purchased them.

You may notice that there are two spellings for Rossetti listed below. I only record what it says and take no responsibility for the Japanese spelling.

Top Row:
    1st and 4th, Man carrying dragon lidded box, 6⅜" (red) $22.50 – 25.00 ea.
    2nd, Georgia map ash tray, (red "H.L. Moore Co.,
        West Yarmouth, Mass")   12.50 – 15.00
    3rd, Knight w/shield ash tray (red H.P. Ardalt, Lenwile
        China #6332)   6.00 – 8.00

Second Row:
    1st, Green floral cigarette box w/two ash trays (red **T** over **M**)   20.00 – 25.00 set
    2nd, Violet cigarette box w/two ash trays, gold "Spring Violets,"
        Rosetti Chicago USA H.P.   25.00 – 30.00 set
    3rd, Dragon decorated cigarette box w/two ash trays (green H.P.)   25.00 – 35.00 set

Third Row:
    1st, Ash tray in Hummel-like design (blue)   10.00 – 12.50
    2nd, Ash tray to match first box in second row   2.00 – 3.00
    3rd, Children in house ash tray (red)   4.00 – 5.00
    4th, Ash tray to match second box in row above   2.50 – 4.00
    5th, Chicken ash tray   5.00 – 6.00
    6th, Ash tray to match third box in second row   3.00 – 5.00

Fourth Row:
    1st, Cigarette box w/ pink rose (red)   10.00 – 12.50
    2nd, "Loop over Great Smokies," "Designed by Burger of Miami"   10.00 – 12.50
    3rd, Diamond ash tray   2.00 – 3.00
    4th, Coal hod match holder w/colonial couple scene (red)   10.00 – 12.50
    5th, Coal hod match holder w/floral scene (green)   10.00 – 12.50
    6th, Moss and Rose cigarette box "H.P. Andrea"   8.00 – 10.00

Fifth Row:
    1st, Pink embossed rose cigarette box (red)   10.00 – 12.50
    2nd, Blue floral cigarette box (gold "Rossetti Chicago")   10.00 – 12.50
    3rd, Swirled floral cigarette box (red Rossetti Chicago H.P.)   10.00 – 12.50
    4th, Florida ash tray (Designed by Burger of Miami, Florida)   12.50 – 15.00

BASKETS, BOOTS, BOOTIES and SHOES

There are more boots here than anyone but a shoe collector could want! However, there are quite a few "shoe" collectors out there who do not care if these are Occupied Japan or not. Shoes are all they care about when it comes to gathering them. I know one collector who makes it even more difficult by trying to find mates for all her single shoes!

Top Row:

1st, Rust shoe w/embossed flower, 2⅜"	$ 6.00 –	8.00
2nd, Blue boot, 3½"	4.00 –	5.00
3rd, Cowboy boot, 4⅜"	6.00 –	8.00
4th, Boot, 6½"	10.00 –	12.50
5th, Tulip boot	6.00 –	8.00
6th, Pink baby boot (Arch emblem)	4.00 –	5.00
7th, George Washington shoe (red #02027)	10.00 –	12.50
8th, Ruffled embossed flower shoe (red cross hair mark)	15.00 –	17.50

Second Row:

1st and 2nd, White shoes w/flowers, 1¾" (red)	2.50 –	4.00 ea.
3rd, Shoe w/rabbit, 2⅜"	6.00 –	8.00
4th, Dutch boy w/shoe	8.00 –	10.00
5th, Lady w/children on embossed floral shoe, 5" high (gold "Chikusa")	65.00 –	75.00
6th, Blue floral shoe	6.00 –	8.00
7th, Baby shoe	4.00 –	5.00
8th, White shoe	2.50 –	4.00
9th, Blue embossed floral shoe, 3½" (red)	7.50 –	10.00

Third Row:

1st, Souvenir Ky. Dam, Ky.	6.00 –	8.00
2nd, Man's shoe	2.00 –	3.00
3rd, Lady's shoe	2.50 –	4.00
4th and 6th, Baby booty planters (Arch emblem)	5.00 –	6.00 ea.
5th, Rabbit shoes	6.00 –	8.00
7th, 9th and 10th, White or black shoes	2.50 –	4.00 ea.
8th, Brown Floral shoe, "Niagara Falls"	7.50 –	10.00

Fourth Row:

1st and 3rd, Heeled shoe, 1¼" and blue pair	2.50 –	4.00 ea.
2nd, Boot (red)	2.50 –	4.00
4th, White w/flowers	4.00 –	5.00
5th, Blue w/pink flower	2.50 –	4.00
6th, 7th, 9th and 11th, Baskets	4.00 –	5.00 ea.
8th, Urn (red)	2.00 –	3.00
10th, Urn w/fruit (red "Pico")	5.00 –	6.00
12th, Shoe (red H. Kato)	2.50 –	4.00

Fifth Row:

1st, 2nd, 6th – 8th, 11th, Baskets	4.00 –	5.00 ea.
3rd and 10th, Wreaths and handle w/ rose	2.50 –	4.00 ea.
5th, Cat w/basket (blue)	5.00 –	6.00
9th, Small basket	2.00 –	3.00
12th, Shoe w/heel	2.00 –	3.00
13th, Ruffled shoe (red **T** over **S** emblem)	4.00 –	5.00

BISQUE

I have had "old-time" antique dealers tell me that the Japanese had lousy quality bisque and that the really nice quality bisque items marked Occupied Japan were actually made in Europe, but marked "Japan" to escape import duties on them. True or not, some of the marked "Occupied Japan" bisque certainly equals the quality of that produced in Europe.

The pastoral couple on the left in the bottom row are exceptionally detailed figurines in all respects.

The couple in the middle of the top row still have the original "29 cents" stickers attached.

Top Row:

1st, Lady w/blue hat, 5" (red)	$15.00 – 17.50
2nd, Lady w/pink hat, 5" (red)	15.00 – 17.50
3rd and 4th, Lady w/fruit and man w/flowers, 6⅜"	40.00 – 50.00 pr.
5th, Man playing flute (red)	15.00 – 17.50
6th, Lady in blue dress (red)	15.00 – 17.50

Second Row:

1st, Girl w/feather in hair, 4⅜" (red **M** over **C**)	12.50 – 15.00
2nd, Man w/rake (red)	12.50 – 15.00
3rd, Bootie	7.50 – 10.00
4th, Colonial man in beige pants (red)	12.50 – 15.00
5th and 6th, Wall pockets, 3⅝" (red)	20.00 – 25.00 pr.

Third Row:

1st and 2nd, Colonial man and lady, 4⅜" (red **M** over **C**)	30.00 – 35.00 pr.
3rd and 4th, Couple w/urns, 5" (red Paulux)	55.00 – 65.00 pr.
5th and 6th, White couple, 4¼" (red)	25.00 – 30.00 pr.

Fourth Row:

1st and 2nd, Pastoral couple by fence, 8⅛" (red)	75.00 – 100.00 pr.
3rd, Lamp couple, 7¼" (red)	40.00 – 50.00
4th and 5th, Musician couple 7⅝" (red)	50.00 – 60.00 pr.

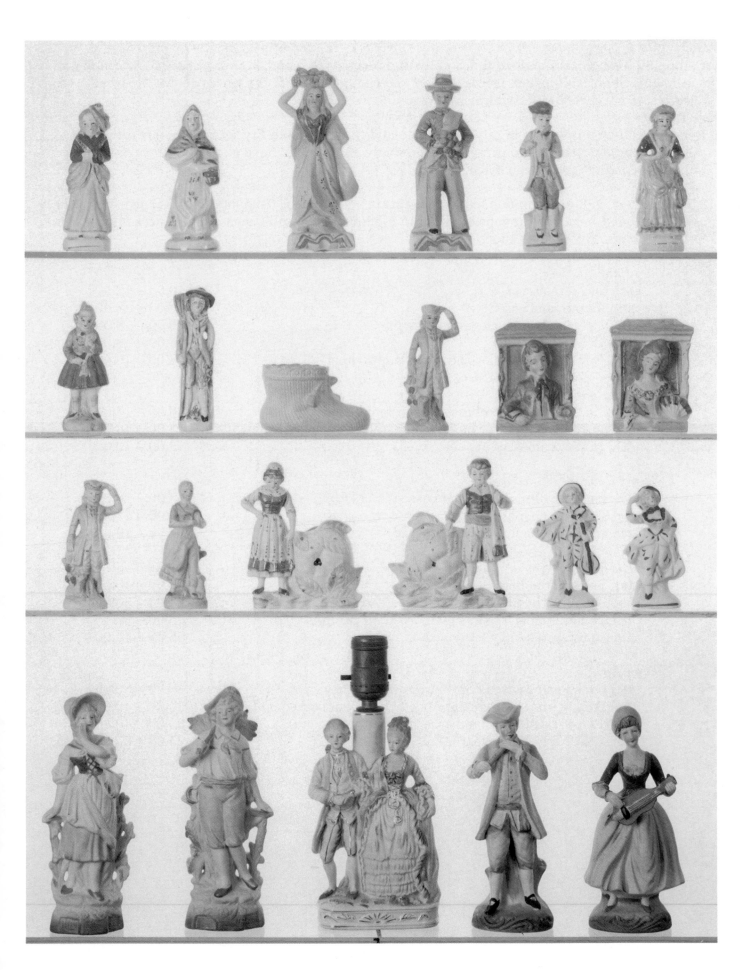

CELLULOID

Celluloid pieces are difficult to find totally undamaged. Remember that prices below are for mint specimens. Slightly damaged pieces will only fetch about half of the prices shown, and badly damaged pieces are rarely collected unless unusual.

Remember that celluloid is highly flammable and that flammability was the major reason for celluloid production being discontinued. Surprisingly, many dolls have survived the ravages of time, but few are found in *mint* condition.

The variety of celluloid animals found could start a small zoo! I see lots of higher prices for these as I shop, but I never see anyone paying the higher price. I sell items at the prices shown below, but they do not "fly" out the shop.

Top Row:

1st, Dog (embossed)	$10.00 – 12.50
2nd, Lamb (embossed)	6.00 – 8.00
3rd, Cow (embossed cloverleaf design)	6.00 – 8.00
4th, Goat (embossed)	6.00 – 8.00
5th, Dog (embossed cloverleaf and paper label)	8.00 – 10.00

Second Row:

1st and 2nd, Goats (embossed cloverleaf design)	6.00 – 8.00 ea.
3rd and 5th, Donkey or horse (embossed cloverleaf design)	8.00 – 10.00 ea.
4th, Horse (embossed)	8.00 – 10.00

Third Row:

1st, 2nd, 6th, Jungle cats (embossed)	8.00 – 10.00 ea.
3rd and 7th, Leopards	10.00 – 12.50 ea.
4th and 5th, Tiger or lion (embossed)	7.50 – 10.00 ea.

Fourth Row:

1st, Snowsuited baby	35.00 – 45.00
2nd, Nodding head donkey (embossed on side)	25.00 – 30.00
3rd, Nodding head donkey (embossed on rump)	25.00 – 30.00
4th, Snowsuited baby (stamped on foot)	35.00 – 50.00

Fifth Row:

1st, Green snowsuited baby (stamped on foot)	25.00 – 30.00
2nd, Yellow snowsuited jointed body baby (embossed on back)	30.00 – 40.00
3rd, Red-headed baby (embossed butterfly emblem)	30.00 – 40.00
4th, U.S. Navy doll (paper label)	25.00 – 30.00

CHILDREN'S DISHES and TOYS

Children's dishes and doll furniture are avidly collected whether or not they are Occupied Japan. Being marked Occupied Japan only adds to their collectabilty because that means that more than one field of collectors are searching for the same pieces. Doll collectors, collectors of children's dishes, and even collectors of miniature items are all buying these pieces. This competition keeps the price soaring especially on complete sets.

The small casserole in the bottom row must have been a promotional item for United China and Glass Company in New Orleans. What irony that the centennial piece for this China company commemorating service from 1850 – 1950 was made in Occupied Japan!

Top Row:
1st, Chair w/roses, 3" (red)	$12.50 – 15.00
2nd, Couch to match, 3" (red)	17.50 – 20.00
3rd, Chair w/roses (on foot)	10.00 – 12.50
4th, Stool to match (brown)	6.00 – 8.00
5th, Dresser	12.50 – 15.00
6th, Colonial scene couch (red)	17.50 – 20.00
7th, Chair to match (red)	12.50 – 15.00

Second Row:
1st and 2nd, Chair and stool w/blue rose (red)	17.50 – 20.00 set
3rd and 4th, Chair w/stool to match	10.00 – 12.50 set
5th and 6th, Chair w/stool to match	12.50 – 15.00 set
7th, Clock chair (red)	12.50 – 15.00
8th – 10th, Lamps (red)	10.00 – 12.50 ea.

Third Row:
1st and 2nd, Bottles	4.00 – 5.00 ea.
3rd, GE Philco refrigerator, 2½"	17.50 – 20.00
4th, Matching cabinet w/dishes, 2¼"	15.00 – 17.50
5th, Matching stove	17.50 – 20.00
6th, Matching dry sink, 2"	10.00 – 12.50
7th, Tub	8.00 – 10.00
8th, Pitcher w/dragon	5.00 – 6.00
9th, Phone (red)	7.50 – 10.00
10th, Cup and saucer (red)	6.00 – 8.00

Fourth Row:
1st, Blue set on tray (red "Isco" in diamond)	17.50 – 20.00
2nd, Tray set (red)	20.00 – 22.50
3rd and 5th, Luster cup (red)	3.00 – 5.00 ea.
4th, Luster sugar w/lid (red)	5.00 – 7.00
5th, Orange luster plate (red)	4.00 – 5.00
6th, Set: tea pot, creamer and sugar	20.00 – 25.00

Fifth Row:
1st and 2nd, Casserole as described above (gold "Meito Norleans China")	50.00 – 75.00
3rd, Tiny set creamer and sugar on tray (red)	6.00 – 8.00
4th, Marching toy soldiers	6.00 – 8.00
5th and 6th, Toy soldiers on horse (red)	6.00 – 8.00 ea.

CHILDREN – MUSICIANS

All of the children displayed here are playing an instrument or singing. I have often wondered why the Japanese so often depicted our children as musicians. They really were obsessed with accordions and mandolins. This was even pre-Lawrence Welk days!

Top Row:

1st, Boy playing accordion (green)	$ 7.50 – 10.00
2nd, Boy playing bass fiddle (green)	7.50 – 10.00
3rd, Boy playing accordion, 5" (red)	10.00 – 12.50
4th and 5th, Girl and boy fiddlers (red)	8.00 – 10.00 ea.
6th and 7th, Boy playing accordion (red)	10.00 – 12.50 ea.
8th, Boy playing mandolin	10.00 – 12.50

Second Row:

1st, Girl playing accordion w/dog, 3⅞" (red flower mark)	10.00 – 12.50
2nd, Boy playing accordion w/dog	10.00 – 12.50
3rd, Girl playing accordion	6.00 – 8.00
4th and 9th, Fiddlers (red)	4.00 – 5.00 ea.
5th and 6th, Boys playing fiddle or mandolin	5.00 – 6.00 ea.
7th, Boy playing accordion (red)	7.50 – 10.00
8th, Boy playing accordion (red)	6.00 – 8.00

Third Row:

1st, Boy playing accordion, 2⅝"	2.00 – 3.00
2nd and 10th, Boy playing accordion (red)	2.50 – 4.00 ea.
3rd and 4th, Girl playing fiddle and boy playing accordion (red)	4.00 – 5.00 ea.
5th – 9th, Musicians (red)	2.50 – 4.00 ea.

Fourth Row:

1st, Accordion playing for chicken, 4⅛"	5.00 – 6.00
2nd, 3rd and 6th, violin playing fence sitters (red)	6.00 – 8.00 ea.
4th and 5th, Boy playing accordion (red)	6.00 – 8.00 ea.
7th, Colonial boy holding violin (red)	6.00 – 8.00
8th, Seated guitar player (red)	4.00 – 5.00

Fifth Row:

1st – 3rd, Robed accordion, mandolin and bass players, 5¾" (red)	12.50 – 15.00 ea.
4th, Girl w/song book, 5¾" (green "Ucagco China" w/emblem)	25.00 – 30.00
5th, Boy playing accordion (brown)	6.00 – 8.00

CHILDREN – SINGLES

A sample of the abundance of child musicians available is continued on this page!

There are probably mates for many of these children, but I have been unable to match them up as yet. Making pairs out of singles is difficult to do in this large collecting field. Note the different colors and sizes of the same figures in the last three rows. This adds to the difficulty of matching pairs.

Top Row:

1st, Flutist, 6" (red)	$12.50 – 15.00
2nd – 4th, Boys playing drums, tuba and horn, 4⅞" (red)	12.50 – 15.00 ea.
5th, Seated flutist	5.00 – 6.00
6th and 8th, Boys playing sax and tuba (red)	8.00 – 10.00 ea.
7th, Boy playing horn (red)	5.00 – 6.00

Second Row:

1st, Tuba player, 3½"	5.00 – 6.00
2nd, Child seated on fence	6.00 – 8.00
3rd, Children on fence (red)	6.00 – 8.00
4th, Boy playing to dogs (red)	7.50 – 10.00
5th, Seated player (red)	6.00 – 8.00
6th – 8th, Seated horn players or drummer	2.50 – 4.00 ea.

Third Row:

1st, 3rd and 6th, Horn player for dogs, chick or goose 2⅝"	2.50 – 4.00 ea.
2nd, Seated w/bird	4.00 – 5.00
4th, Seated on fence, 2⅜" (red)	2.50 – 4.00
5th, Girl w/yellow dress	6.00 – 8.00
7th, Girl w/ book (blue)	6.00 – 8.00
8th, Girl w/umbrella, 4¼"	6.00 – 8.00

Fourth Row:

1st, Seated w/duck (red)	10.00 – 12.50
2nd and 5th, Girl on fence or w/umbrella and dog	6.00 – 8.00 ea.
3rd, Seated girl, 4¾"	10.00 – 12.50
4th, Seated girl (slightly smaller), 4½"	10.00 – 12.50
6th, Girl w/umbrella (red)	4.00 – 5.00
7th, Seated girl w/watering can (bookend), 3⅝" (red)	12.50 – 15.00

Fifth Row:

1st – 3rd, "Dolly Dimples" w/rabbit or duck (red cross in cloverleaf)	10.00 – 12.50 ea.
4th, Girl holding doll, 4¼"	12.50 – 15.00
5th, Girl w/cloak (H.P. red)	6.00 – 8.00
6th – 8th, Girls w/rabbit or chick	4.00 – 5.00 ea.
9th, Girl w/pocket book, 4⅛"	7.50 – 10.00

CUP and SAUCERS

The next four pictures show a wide selection of cup and saucers. Some are of excellent quality and others are poorly made as is the case of most items collected from Occupied Japan.

We have turned some of the cups and saucers to show off their colorful interiors. Many of the sets shown in this section are ones that go with sets of dinnerware.

The three "Trimont" cup and saucer sets in the top row were found with the orange set pictured in the middle of the top row on page 37 in the *The Collector's Encyclopedia of Occupied Japan, 4th Series*.

Top Row:
    1st – 3rd, Sets of green, blue and pink "Trimont China HP" $17.50 – 20.00 ea.

Second Row:
    1st, "Capo di Monte" type plate (red)   10.00 – 12.50
    2nd, Set, w/dancing girls (red)   20.00 – 25.00
    3rd, Set, w/dancing girls (blue **SGK** basket w/wreath H.P.)   25.00 – 30.00
    4th, Demitasse, 1¼" (Ardalt H.P. Lenwile China 6195)   20.00 – 22.50

Third Row:
    1st, Set, red hearts w/black trim (red)   7.50 – 10.00
    2nd, Set, blue w/floral (gold "Chugai China" w/mountain emblem)   10.00 – 12.50
    3rd, Set, black w/gold trim (gold "Ucagco China" w/emblem)   10.00 – 12.50
    4th, Set, blue and white (blue)   10.00 – 12.50

Fourth Row:
    1st, Set, (orange "Diamond China")   7.50 – 10.00
    2nd, Set, black and white checkerboard border (blue)   4.00 – 5.00
    3rd Set, blue rim floral (blue)   5.00 – 6.00
    4th Set, Florida souvenir (red C over M)   8.00 – 10.00

Fifth Row:
    1st, Set, ladies w/red rim (Ardalt Lenwile China 6521)   20.00 – 22.50
    2nd, Set, yellow rim flower (gold "Gold Castle" R.E.G.)   7.50 – 10.00
    3rd, Demitasse white floral (gold "Chata China")   8.00 – 10.00
    4th, Set, (red "Chugai China" w/mountain emblem)   7.50 – 10.00

CUP and SAUCERS (Cont.)

For you collectors who specialize in demitasse sets, feast your eyes on these!

Top Row:

1st, Demitasse, light yellow w/floral (red)	$ 5.00 – 6.00
2nd, Demitasse, Oriental scene w/lady (red)	8.00 – 10.00
3rd, Demitasse, white w/flowers (red)	6.00 – 8.00
4th, Demitasse, cream w/basket weave rim "Great Smokey Mountains" (red)	8.00 – 10.00
5th, Demitasse, "Moss Rose" type (green "Orata China" w/ interlocking **OC** in wreath emblem)	8.00 – 10.00

Second Row:

1st, Set, white w/pink (red "Hadson Chinaware" w/anchor mark)	6.00 – 8.00
2nd, Set, white w/roses (red "Merit")	6.00 – 8.00
3rd, Set, white w/leaves (red)	4.00 – 5.00
4th, Set, fancy, footed cup w/daisy ("Orata China" w/interlocking **OC**)	7.50 – 10.00

Third Row:

1st, Demitasse, black w/lacy flower (green **HB** in diamond)	10.00 – 12.50
2nd, Demitasse, fancy w/gold, 2⅝" ("Shofu China" H.P.)	15.00 – 17.50
3rd, Demitasse, hexagonal (red **M** over **B**)	12.50 – 15.00
4th, Demitasse, small dragon (red)	10.00 – 12.50
5th, Demitasse, large dragon (blue)	12.50 – 15.00

Fourth Row:

1st, Demitasse, green stripe (gold "Ucagco China" w/emblem)	12.50 – 15.00
2nd, Demitasse, Colonial scene (H.P. "Shofu China")	20.00 – 22.50
3rd, Demitasse, black and orange floral (red **M** over **B**)	8.00 – 10.00
4th, Demitasse, Oriental house scene (red)	4.00 – 5.00
5th, Demitasse, wine rim (red elephant head **A**)	6.00 – 8.00

Fifth Row:

1st, Demitasse, rust swirl (gold)	7.50 – 10.00
2nd, Demitasse, blue rim (red)	5.00 – 6.00
3rd, Demitasse, orange luster rim (red)	5.00 – 6.00
4th, Demitasse, rose w/gold (red)	6.00 – 8.00
5th, Demitasse, rust curved in top (red H. Kato)	10.00 – 12.50

CUP and SAUCERS (Cont.)

There were many odd saucers in a collection I purchased and a few of the more eye pleasing ones are shown in the top two rows.

Top Row:

1st, Saucer, black w/orange flower (red)	$ 2.00 – 3.00
2nd, Saucer, green w/orange star shaped flower (red H.P. "Gold China")	2.00 – 3.00
3rd, Saucer, black Iris (red)	2.00 – 3.00
4th, Saucer, green w/gold stripe (red)	2.00 – 3.00

Second Row:

1st, Saucer, pine cone on grey (red Burger of Miami)	2.00 – 3.00
2nd, Saucer, rust, square ("Trimont China")	2.00 – 3.00
3rd, Saucer, green w/rose (red)	2.00 – 3.00
4th, Saucer, yellow w/flowers (red)	2.00 – 3.00

Third Row:

1st, Demitasse, 1½", violet flowers (red)	6.00 – 8.00
2nd, Miniature, 1", orange rim, souvenir Army Navy Hospital (red)	6.00 – 8.00
3rd, Miniature, white floral (green)	7.50 – 10.00
4th, Miniature, squared cup (red **Y** emblem)	8.00 – 10.00
5th, Miniature, scalloped, six sided (orange)	6.00 – 8.00

Fourth Row:

1st, Miniature, pink blush (w/cross in world marking)	10.00 – 12.50
2nd, Miniature, square floral saucer (orange)	4.00 – 5.00
3rd, Same as 2nd in Row 3 except blue rim and not souvenir	4.00 – 5.00
4th, Miniature, souvenir N.Y.C. and Statue of Liberty (red)	6.00 – 8.00
5th, Miniature, green rim floral (blue "Baby China")	5.00 – 6.00

Fifth Row:

1st, Miniature, blue rim, ⅞" (orange)	6.00 – 8.00
2nd, Miniature, green rim (orange)	5.00 – 6.00
3rd, Miniature, square footed cup (red)	6.00 – 8.00
4th, Miniature, gold /white "Cherokee Indian Reservation, N.C.," (red)	6.00 – 8.00
5th, Demitasse, "New Orleans, La., Courtyard, Governor Claiborne House" (red)	8.00 – 10.00

CUP and SAUCERS (Cont.) and DECORATIVE PLATES

We turned the cups on the bottom row so you could see their colorful interiors. This is typical of many "Occupied Japan" cups. Unfortunately, the information on marks for the fifth row was omitted in my notes made at the photography session. Writing this one year later, I can only tell you that they were Occupied Japan.

Top Row:

1st, Plate, "Niagara Falls"	$ 7.50 — 10.00
2nd, Plate, "Souvenir of Cheyenne, Wyoming"	4.00 — 5.00
3rd, Plate, rust dragon, CK emblem	5.00 — 6.00
4th, Saucer, blue striped, (red "Aiyo China")	2.00 — 3.00
5th, Cup, grey, silver and gold, footed	6.00 — 8.00

Second Row:

1st, Hanging plate, "Macinaw Isl., Mich." (red)	2.50 — 4.00
2nd, Plate, Niagara Falls (red)	4.00 — 5.00
3rd, Plate, "Parliament Building, Winnipeg" (red)	4.00 — 5.00
4th, Plate, "New Orleans" (red)	6.00 — 8.00
5th. Blue tulip shaped cup, "Merit China"	8.00 — 10.00
6th, White w/gold four footed cup (gold "Ucagco China" w/emblem)	8.00 — 10.00

Third Row:

1st, Plate, windmill scene (red)	2.50 — 4.00
2nd, Hanging plate, "Castalia, Ohio" (red)	2.50 — 4.00
3rd, Cup and saucer, squared, black	8.00 — 10.00
4th, Demitasse cup only (blue)	5.00 — 6.00
5th, Demitasse cup only w/ dragon (red)	7.50 — 10.00
6th, Miniature set, w/scene	4.00 — 5.00
7th, Miniature set, blue rim "Grand Canyon" (red)	6.00 — 8.00

Fourth Row:

1st, Miniature set, green rim (red)	4.00 — 5.00
2nd Plate to match (red)	2.50 — 4.00
3rd, Miniature set, rust rim (red)	2.50 — 4.00
4th, Hanging plate, "Cherokee Indian Reservation, N.C."	4.00 — 5.00
5th, Miniature set, white floral (red)	5.00 — 6.00
6th, Plate, matching square white floral (red)	2.50 — 4.00
7th, Miniature set, ¾", "Souvenir of Las Vegas, N.M."	6.00 — 8.00
8th, Cup, four footed, black (gold "Ucagco China" w/emblem)	10.00 — 12.50

Fifth Row:

See paragraph above!

1st, Cup only	4.00 — 5.00
2nd – 5th Cups only	8.00 — 10.00 ea.

DECORATIVE ITEMS – PLATES and BOWLS

There are many decorative "Occupied Japan" plates that would sell for double the price (or more) if they were marked "Germany," "Austria" or even "Bavaria." Quality workmanship is often disdained because it is Japanese. Oddly enough, collectors do not attach the same stigma to "Nippon" which means Japan. "Nippon" marked items only have an age factor of a minimum fifteen years earlier than Occupied Japan.

Another problem you may run into with decorative plates is noticing that the MIOJ marks were scratched off! I have never heard of any one removing an European mark, but "old fashioned dealers" still feel MIOJ merchandise is beneath the dignity of their shops. Thus they removed or at least attempted to remove the now valuable MIOJ mark!

Top Row:
1st, Cabin scene w/five chickens (red)	17.50 – 20.00
2nd and 3rd, Plums or cherries (gold "Ucagco China" w/emblem)	20.00 – 25.00 ea.
4th, Sailing ship (red)	17.50 – 20.00

Second Row:
1st, Fish dish (circle **K**)	10.00 – 12.50
2nd, Lake scene w/two buildings (red hand painted)	6.00 – 8.00
3rd, Floral handled relish (green H.P.)	6.00 – 8.00
4th, Lake scene w/two swans (red H.P.)	10.00 – 12.50
5th, Birds of paradise w/luster edge (red)	12.50 – 15.00

Third Row:
1st – 5th, Geisha girl plates, all marked (red "No 6078 Ardalt H. P.")	20.00 – 25.00 ea.

Fourth Row:
1st, Brown leaf w/handle, (embossed MIOJ)	8.00 – 10.00
2nd, Brown, curled finger handle, holes for reed handle (embossed MIOJ)	8.00 – 10.00
3rd, Brown divided dish (gold **M** over **O**)	4.00 – 5.00
4th, Brown w/grapes and four holes for handles (embossed)	6.00 – 8.00

DECORATIVE ITEMS – (Cont.)

Top Row:

1st, Yellow flower, (gold "Ucagco China" w/emblem, "Floral B")	$12.50 – 15.00
2nd, Scalloped edge fruit w/peach and plums (red)	7.50 – 10.00
3rd, Purple leaf (red AJ808)	6.00 – 8.00
4th, Orange flowers "Aiyo" (brown)	12.50 – 15.00
5th, Oval lattice bowl	10.00 – 12.50

Second Row:

1st, Rose floral dish (**W** in wreath)	4.00 – 5.00
2nd, "Cup of Gold" (gold Rossetti, Chicago USA, H.P.)	10.00 – 12.50
3rd, Lattice ladies w/child (red)	17.50 – 20.00
4th, Shell w/couple (blue elephant **A** symbol)	6.00 – 8.00
5th, Blue edge floral (red)	8.00 – 10.00
6th, Red edge floral (red)	8.00 – 10.00

Third Row:

1st, Floral, (blue "Narumi China")	2.50 – 4.00
2nd, Leaf relish (gold "Ucagco China" w/emblem)	10.00 – 12.50
3rd, Latticed, floral bowl	6.00 – 8.00
4th, Floral leaf (gold H.P. Rossetti)	7.50 – 10.00
5th, Tree scene (gold "Ucagco China" w/emblem)	5.00 – 6.00
6th, Dog (green H.P. Rossetti)	10.00 – 12.50
7th, Latticed fruit w/grapes and peach (H.P. **W** in wreath)	8.00 – 10.00

Fourth Row:

1st, Floral leaf	2.50 – 4.00
2nd, Latticed floral (red)	6.00 – 8.00
3rd, Latticed fruit and flowers (red H.P.)	10.00 – 12.50
4th, Square floral bowl (red)	6.00 – 8.00
5th, Square, handled floral plate (gold Rossetti)	8.00 – 10.00
6th, Square, handled floral plate (H.P. shield w/**JA** inside)	8.00 – 10.00

DINNERWARE

I was astonished to learn just how many sets of Occupied Japan china are available that were never used or only used occasionally. In early July 1990, an article on Occupied Japan appeared in many of the nation's newspapers. The reporter had interviewed me as well as others about the phenomenon of collecting this ware. The article was slightly inaccurate and did not point out that most MIOJ pieces are still priced cheaply. Instead, the emphasis was on the highly priced items. No mention was made regarding "Occupied Japan" dinnerware patterns and how **uncollectible** they are, at present. Therefore, I started receiving calls on a Sunday morning in July and it was the middle of August before the calls had stopped coming regularly!

Most of the calls were about eight or twelve place settings of dinnerware that people wanted to sell for big bucks! After all, the article said if it was made in Occupied Japan, it was valuable. All in all, there were over fifty calls wanting to sell sets of dinnerware. Most were unnamed patterns. (It would be great if someone could put pattern names for these sets together.) Had I known there would be that many calls…!

Amazingly, whole Occupied Japan dinnerware sets do not sell easily! People, in general, do not buy sets for which they cannot find replacements, or at least that has been my experience with Occupied Japan dinnerware. Individual pieces are also hard to sell unless someone is looking for that particular pattern.In that event, you will pay a premium to get cups, dinner plates and serving pieces which were not sold with all sets. Therefore, if you add up the cost of individual pieces, you will find that the parts are more costly than the whole set if bought at once.

The dinnerware on page 41 has apples or crab apples for a design. It is all marked in gold lettering "Ucagco China" w/emblem MIOJ.

Top Row:
1st, Sugar w/lid	$ 10.00 –	12.50
2nd, 8" vegetable bowl (standing up)	15.00 –	17.50
3rd, Cereal bowl	5.00 –	6.00
4th, Creamer	6.00 –	8.00

Second Row:
1st, Platter, 15"	20.00 –	25.00

Third Row:
1st, Cup and saucer	7.50 –	10.00
2nd, Bread and butter plate	2.50 –	4.00
3rd, Dinner plate	20.00 –	22.50

Prices For Occupied Japan Dinnerware Sets

Set for four including: cups, saucers, plates in 3 sizes, berry and soup bowls, creamer and covered sugar	175.00 – 200.00
Set for 6 including all of above and cereal bowls, gravy boat and small platter	225.00 – 250.00
Set for 8 including all of above and 2 platters	275.00 – 300.00
Set for 12 including all of above and adding covered casserole and turkey platter	400.00 – 450.00

DINNERWARE – Blue Willow

People who are not collectors recognize the name Blue Willow. It is easily the most widely known pattern of Japanese dinnerware whether it is marked MIOJ or not. The quality of Blue Willow dinnerware varies greatly. Some is very porous and stains very easily, while other pieces are of excellent quality.

Prices are for the pieces shown on page 43 only!

Top Row:

1st – 7th, All items are marked blue MIOJ with a crown emblem:

Saucer	$ 2.00 – 3.00
Dinner plate, 9"	12.50 – 15.00
Sugar w/lid	17.50 – 20.00
Salad plate, 7"	6.00 – 8.00
Creamer	12.50 – 15.00
Cereal bowl, 5¾"	12.50 – 15.00
Berry bowl, 4½"	10.00 – 12.50

Second Row:

1st, Dinner plate w/red and yellow flowers (blue house mark MIOJ)	17.50 – 20.00
2nd, Same, berry bowl	10.00 – 12.50
3rd, Bread and butter (blue)	4.00 – 5.00
4th, Dinner plate (blue)	10.00 – 12.50
5th, Saucer (blue "Nasco")	2.00 – 3.00

Third Row:

1st, Cup and saucer (blue)	15.00 – 17.50
2nd, Platter, 12" (blue **R** w/shield **P**)	40.00 – 50.00
3rd, Berry bowl (blue crown w/**M** inside and cross on top)	10.00 – 12.50
4th, Platter, 12" (very porous) (blue)	25.00 – 30.00

DINNERWARE – MISCELLANEOUS

Most of the pieces shown on page 45 are items from large dinnerware sets. Most often you will only find partial sets, so here are a few individual pieces. Prices for complete dinnerware sets are found on page 40.

Top Row:

1st, Sugar w/lid, birds on luster glaze (red **KA** in diamond)	$15.00 – 17.50
2nd, Creamer, floral as on sugar (**A** in circle "Aichi China")	8.00 – 10.00
3rd, Sugar w/lid, (same as creamer above)	15.00 – 17.50
4th, Sugar w/lid (Orange "Ucagco China" w/emblem)	10.00 – 12.50
5th, Creamer to match	6.00 – 8.00
6th, Saucer to match	2.00 – 3.00

Second Row:

1st, Creamer (red)	6.00 – 8.00
2nd, Sugar w/lid to match	10.00 – 12.50
3rd, Berry bowl ("Adling China")	4.00 – 5.00
4th, Berry bowl ("Noritake" **M** in wreath)	

Third Row:

1st, Creamer (red)	6.00 – 8.00
2nd, Sugar w/lid to match	10.00 – 12.50
3rd, Sugar w/lid ("Noritake" w/unusual handles)	15.00 – 17.50
4th, Sugar w/lid (SGK China)	10.00 – 12.50
5th, Creamer to match	6.00 – 8.00

Fourth Row:

1st, Creamer, small flowers (gold "Ucagco China" w/emblem)	10.00 – 12.50
2nd, Sugar w/lid (red crown w/"Rossetti Chicago USA Hand Painted")	15.00 – 17.50
3rd, Creamer to match	8.00 – 10.00
4th, Cup (red "Hadson Chinaware" w/anchor)	4.00 – 5.00
5th, Creamer (gold **A** in circle "Aichi China")	7.50 – 10.00

Fifth Row:

1st, Snack set (red **G** in ivy)	12.50 – 15.00
2nd, Snack set (red)	12.50 – 15.00
3rd, Snack set w/cup (red **G** in ivy)	12.50 – 15.00

ELVES and GNOMES

It's fun to find a member of one of these sets that you do not already have. Usually you find the same members over and over. It took me years to find the elf riding the frog in the second row. All of the other members of this set that I have seen ride insects, but this one is aboard a frog!

The bottom row are figures made to look like wood carvings. All are musicians except the third one who has a pipe.

Top Row:

1st, One handed orator gnome, 5⅛"	$12.50	15.00
2nd, Tired old gnome	10.00	12.50
3rd, Red elf w/pot (red cross hair in circle)	12.50	15.00
4th, Elf w/log (brown)	10.00	12.50
5th, Red elf w/planter	12.50	15.00
6th, Gnome w/basket	12.50	15.00

Second Row:

1st, Leaf hat recliner (red cross hair in circle)	10.00	12.50
2nd and 3rd, Leaf reclining pair (blue)	20.00	25.00 pr.
4th, Elf on frog (blue)	20.00	25.00
5th, Elf on caterpillar	12.50	15.00

Third Row:

1st – 3rd and 6th, Purple suited elves (red/red cross hair in circle)	12.50	15.00 ea.
4th and 5th, Green suited elves (red cross hair in circle)	12.50	15.00 ea.

Fourth Row:

1st and 3rd, Orange suited sitters (red)	10.00	12.50 ea.
2nd and 4th, Purple or blue recliners (red)	10.00	12.50 ea.
5th, Old lady gnome, 2½" (blue)	4.00	5.00
6th, Old lady gnome, 3¾" (red)	6.00	8.00
7th and 8th, Old man gnome (red)	6.00	8.00 ea.

Fifth Row:

1st and 3rd, Wooden looking figurines (red)	6.00	8.00 ea.
2nd and 4th – 8th, Wooden looking musicians	6.00	8.00 ea.

ETHNIC REPRESENTATIONS

Ethnic groups represented by figurines in this time period were multitudinous. Black and American Indian figurines are now collected by many. Most of these figurines were made as stereotypes, so many have been destroyed down through the years. (I have not found many black stereotypes recently.) Blacks are only represented here as musicians. I personally know of some black people who used to make it their mission in life to remove from the market as many stereotypical personifications as possible.

On the bottom row is an organ grinder. Unless he's Italian, I have no idea how he got in this photo.

Top Row:

1st, Indian planter, 7⅛" (red mountain symbol w/smeared writing "Yamashira"?)	$20.00 – 25.00
2nd, American Indian ash tray (embossed)	10.00 – 12.50
3rd, Black drummer, 5" (red)	35.00 – 40.00
4th, Black horn player, 6¼"	40.00 – 45.00
5th, Cowboy ash tray (embossed "Privue Prod, Inc. c. 1950)	2.50 – 4.00
6th, Mexican on donkey, 8¼" (red)	25.00 – 30.00

Second Row:

1st – 5th, Black musicians, 2¾" (red or black)	15.00 – 17.50 ea.
6th and 7th, Dutch girl and boy (red)	12.50 – 15.00 pr.
8th and 9th, Single Dutch shakers (red)	5.00 – 6.00 ea.

Third Row:

1st and 2nd, Dutch girl and boy w/bucket on string, 4¼"	20.00 – 25.00 pr.
3rd Dutch girl bell	12.50 – 15.00
4th, Seated Dutch girl	12.50 – 15.00
5th, Seated Dutch boy (**M** in circle)	12.50 – 15.00
6th, Small Dutch girl (red)	4.00 – 5.00
7th, Dutch boy (red)	5.00 – 6.00
8th, Single Dutch shaker	5.00 – 6.00

Fourth Row:

1st, American Indian lady, 4¼" (red)	6.00 – 8.00
2nd, American Indian in canoe (red)	10.00 – 12.50
3rd, Cowgirl on horse	6.00 – 8.00
4th, Cowboy or Mexican drummer (red)	5.00 – 6.00
5th, Cowgirl	7.50 – 10.00
6th, Mexican guitar player	5.00 – 6.00
7th, Cowboy	7.50 – 10.00

Fifth Row:

1st and 2nd, Indian couple, 6⅛" (red)	20.00 – 25.00 pr.
3rd, Organ grinder (red)	20.00 – 22.50
4th, American Indian chief, 5¹⁄₁₆" (red)	15.00 – 17.50
5th, Hawaiian girl w/guitar (red)	10.00 – 12.50
6th and 7th, Hula girls (red)	7.50 – 10.00 ea.

FIGURINES – DOUBLES

All these figurines are couples (man and woman in those days). You may find that these occur in mirrored image pairs, sometimes referred to as end or mantel pairs (one for each end of the mantel); however, I have only found one of each of these. Note the abundance of Colonial attired figures throughout this section.

Top Row:

1st, Colonial couple in blue, 4¾" (red)	$12.50 –	15.00
2nd, Couple w/man in yellow cape	20.00 –	22.50
3rd, Couple w/hats (red)	12.50 –	15.00
4th, Man whispering in her ear (red H.P.)	25.00 –	30.00
5th, Fence sitters (red)	12.50 –	15.00
6th, Mandolin wooing	12.50 –	15.00

Second Row:

1st, Seated couple w/book, 3⅜" (red)	10.00 –	12.50
2nd, 4th and 7th, Couples (red)	10.00 –	12.50 ea.
3rd, 5th and 8th Couples	10.00 –	12.50 ea.
6th, Removing or putting on coat (red)	12.50 –	15.00

Third Row:

1st, Dancing couple, 7¼" (red **L.D.** in flower face emblem)	30.00 –	35.00
2nd, Cinderella and Prince Charming 8¼" ("Maruyama"; red)	100.00 –	125.00
3rd, Couple, 7⅛" (red "Moriyama" basket emblem)	30.00 –	35.00
4th, Dancers, 6⅛" (red)	25.00 –	30.00

Fourth Row:

1st, Colonial seated, 3⅝" (red)	7.50 –	10.00
2nd, 5th and 7th, Couples (red)	10.00 –	12.50 ea.
3rd and 4th, Couples, 5½" (red)	20.00 –	22.50 ea.
6th, Wooden looking couple (red)	15.00 –	17.50

FIGURINES – DOUBLES and GROUPS

The couple on sleds in the top row is one of my customers favorite type figurines! I find them only occasionally. Years ago, these seemed to be rather common, but collections have depleted that supply.

As I have stated in earlier editions, finding Occupied Japan figurines with more than two people on them is unusual. The only different one I have found in the last five years is shown in the fourth row.

Top Row:
    1st and 3rd, Sled couple, 5¾" $150.00 – 175.00 pr.
    2nd, Courting couple, 6¼"   40.00 – 50.00

Second Row:
    1st and 4th, Couples, 5½" (red)   17.50 – 20.00 ea.
    2nd and 3rd, Couples   20.00 – 25.00 ea.

Third Row:
    1st and 3rd, Couples, 4" (red)   17.50 – 20.00 ea.
    2nd, Couple (red)   10.00 – 12.50
    4th, Couple, 5" (red)   17.50 – 20.00
    5th, Couple (blue **L.D.** in flower face emblem) 20.00 – 25.00

Fourth Row:
    1st, Man in hat proposing or propositioning, 3¾" 15.00 – 17.50
    2nd, Triple figure (red)   15.00 – 20.00
    3rd, Seated couple w/dog (red "Maruyama")   30.00 – 40.00
    4th, Musician lady and fellow (red) (probably "Maruyama";
       see row 5, 1st)   20.00 – 25.00
    5th, Couple at piano   12.50 – 15.00
    6th, Couple (red)   12.50 – 15.00

Fifth Row:
    1st, Cellist lady and fellow, 3½" ("Maruyama") 20.00 – 25.00
    2nd and 7th, Couple w/dog and skirt lifter (red) 12.50 – 15.00 ea.
    3rd and 5th, Couples, 2⅜" (red)   4.00 –   5.00 ea.
    4th, Dancers (red "Yamaha")   6.00 –   8.00
    6th, Couple (red)   5.00 –   6.00

FIGURINES – DOUBLES and PAIRS

Note that pairs of double figurines are mirrored (opposite) images of each other. There is a full gamut of high and low quality figurines represented on this page.

Top Row:

1st, Couple at piano, 5½" (gold **L.D.** in flower face emblem)	$50.00 – 65.00
2nd, Lady w/fan and man w/hat, 6⅜" (red H.P.)	40.00 – 50.00
3rd, Man wooing lady w/flute, 6⅞"	50.00 – 65.00

Second Row:

1st, Couple w/lady playing mandolin, 5½" (red)	40.00 – 50.00
2nd, Couple w/man playing mandolin (red anchor mark)	20.00 – 25.00
3rd, Seated couple	10.00 – 12.50
4th, Couple	17.50 – 20.00

Third Row:

1st and 2nd, Colonial pair, 4⅛" (red)	25.00 – 30.00 pr.
3rd and 4th, Couple pair (H.P.)	30.00 – 35.00 pr.
5th and 6th, Mandolin playing man pair, 4⅜"	35.00 – 40.00 pr.

Fourth Row:

1st and 2nd, Larger version of pair above, 5" (red)	40.00 – 50.00 pr.
3rd and 4th, Couple w/man in red/white/blue pants, 3¾" (red)	17.50 – 20.00 pr.
5th and 6th, Slightly different sizes painted similarly	17.50 – 20.00 ea.

Fifth Row:

1st, Dancing couple, 3⅛" (red)	8.00 – 10.00
2nd – 5th, Couples, 2¼" to 2½" (red)	5.00 – 6.00 ea.
6th, Couple (crown emblem)	12.50 – 15.00
7th, Couple seated	12.50 – 15.00

FIGURINES – PAIRS

Finding pairs that I have not shown in my previous four books is getting to be as big a chore as finding undamaged pairs!

Remember that individual figurines are half the lowest price of the pair!

Top Row:

1st and 2nd, Pair w/blue coated man and lady with panniers, 6¼"	$ 45.00 –	60.00
3rd and 4th, Pair w/pink and gray, 7½" ("Moriyama")	40.00 –	50.00
5th and 6th, Colonial pair in yellow, 8" (red)	50.00 –	65.00

Second Row:

1st and 2nd, Pair dancers, 5¼" (red)	30.00 –	35.00
3rd and 4th, Pair w/baskets, 5½" (red)	35.00 –	40.00
5th and 6th, Dutch pair, 4⅛" (H.P.)	20.00 –	22.50
7th and 8th, Colonial pair, 5½" (red)	30.00 –	35.00

Third Row:

1st and 2nd, Pair musicians, 10⅛"	95.00 –	110.00
3rd and 4th, Pair in yellow, 10" ("Paulux")	110.00 –	125.00
5th and 6th, Pair Dutch peasants, 8¼" (red)	50.00 –	65.00

Fourth Row:

1st and 2nd, Colonial pair w/man playing mandolin, 6⅛" (H.P.)	40.00 –	50.00
3rd and 4th, Colonial pair w/man holding mandolin, 6½" (red)	45.00 –	60.00
5th and 6th, Dutch pair (red)	17.50 –	20.00
7th and 8th, Fancily laced pair (red patent 1948)	35.00 –	50.00

FIGURINES – LADY DANCERS and SINGLE WOMEN

Ballerinas are a popular collectible. Those with skirts made of netting are the most desirable, but these are often damaged. A little damage on these seems not to matter to avid collectors, but a lot of damage is not tolerated.

Some of the dancers may have had partners, but not when I found them.

Did you ever wonder why many of the ladies depicted by the Japanese seem to be leaning into a strong head wind? Note the fourth lady in the bottom row. I have always called this style "wind swept" for lack of a better description. Of course I have never been able to figure out that pose leaning backward and holding the hat and the hem of the dress. Perhaps they are about to swoon? That pose can be seen on several different figurines.

Top Row:
1st, Arms behind head pose, 5" (red)	$15.00 – 17.50
2nd, Holding hem and hat (red)	17.50 – 20.00
3rd, Ballerina with net dress, 5¾"	35.00 – 40.00
4th, Holding hem of dress (red)	10.00 – 12.50
5th, Dancing planter, 5½"	12.50 – 15.00

Second Row:
1st, Green skirted, 3½" ("Hadson" w/anchor mark)	10.00 – 12.50
2nd, White skirted	5.00 – 6.00
3rd, Green and white dress (red)	6.00 – 8.00
4th, Ballerina (red)	12.50 – 15.00
5th, Blue ruffled skirt (red)	7.50 – 10.00
6th, White skirted w/rust top	4.00 – 5.00

Third Row:
1st, Ballerina, 4¾" (red "Orion" Pat #7672)	35.00 – 40.00
2nd, Ballerina (red cross hair mark)	15.00 – 17.50
3rd, Ballerina (red)	10.00 – 12.50
4th, Ballerina (red #510 H.P.)	17.50 – 20.00
5th, Ballerina w/ purple dress (blue **R** in pallet emblem)	25.00 – 30.00

Fourth Row:
1st, 3rd and 6th, Small dancers, 2½" (red)	5.00 – 6.00 ea.
2nd, Pink, holding dress hems (red)	8.00 – 10.00
4th, Orange skirt ("Pico")	5.00 – 6.00
5th, Blue top	5.00 – 6.00
7th, White w/gold (red)	6.00 – 8.00

Fifth Row:
1st and 6th, Yellow skirt, 3½"	8.00 – 10.00 ea.
2nd and 5th, Slightly different decorations, 5⅜" (red)	20.00 – 25.00 ea.
3rd, Hands behind head pose (Brown)	15.00 – 17.50
4th, Wind swept lady (red)	12.50 – 15.00

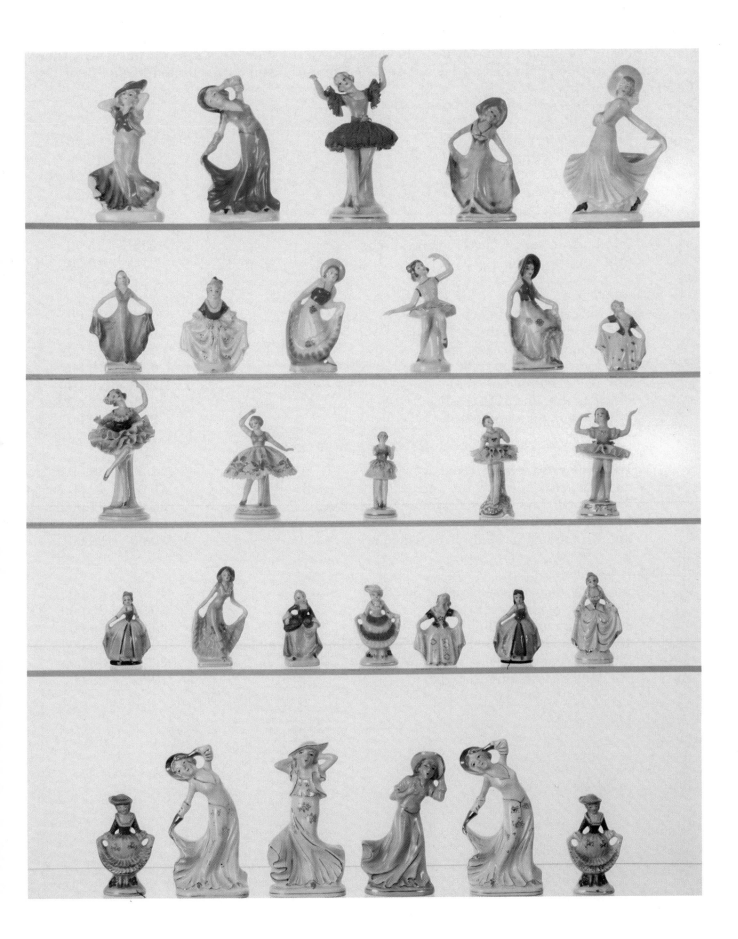

FIGURINES – SINGLE LADIES

In all likelihood there are male companions for most of these ladies, but I have been unable to find them. Generally speaking, pairs are more in demand than the individual pieces. That is why there is a premium price on pairs. However, a lady called recently who only collected female figurines. She should enjoy this page!

Top Row:

1st, Lady w/tambourine, 4¾"	$ 6.00 – 8.00
2nd, Lady in white and gold (red)	8.00 – 10.00
3rd, Lady w/rust top (red)	6.00 – 8.00
4th, Lady w/feathered hat, 6"	10.00 – 12.50
5th, Mexican lady, 7¼" (red "Ucagco China" w/emblem)	35.00 – 40.00
6th, Lady holding hat (red)	10.00 – 12.50
7th, Lady in yellow and blue dress (red)	12.50 – 15.00
8th, Lady w/basket	8.00 – 10.00

Second Row:

1st, Surprised expression, 5" (red)	12.50 – 15.00
2nd, Holding green dress	10.00 – 12.50
3rd, Yellow top w/bow in hair	5.00 – 6.00
4th, Lady w/rust top (red)	6.00 – 8.00
5th, Lady holding hat (red)	12.50 – 15.00
6th, 7th, 9th, and 10th, Ladies (red)	10.00 – 12.50 ea.
8th, Lady in pink and blue	2.50 – 4.00

Third Row:

1st, Lady w/Scottie, 4½" (red)	12.50 – 15.00
2nd and 7th, Lady in white and seated lady (red)	10.00 – 12.50 ea.
3rd and 4th, Ladies in yellow floral skirts (red)	15.00 – 17.50 ea.
5th, Lady reading book, 5"	22.50 – 25.00
6th, Crinoline dress lady, 5⅝" (red #526)	30.00 – 35.00

Fourth Row:

1st, Lady w/crown and scepter, 8⅛" (blue)	40.00 – 45.00
2nd, Lady reading book, 8⅜"	30.00 – 35.00
3rd, Buxom lady holding fan, 9¾"	45.00 – 50.00
4th, Dutch lady w/flowers, 10⅛" ("Ucagco China" w/emblem)	40.00 – 50.00
5th, Girl w/apron, 8¼"	30.00 – 35.00
6th, Well endowed dancer (red)	20.00 – 25.00

FIGURINES – MEN

As with the ladies, there are probably companions for most of the men shown here, but I was unable to match them.

Top Row:

1st, Blue boy, 7⅝"	$30.00 – 35.00
2nd, Man in striped pants (red "Ucagco China" w/emblem)	20.00 – 25.00
3rd, Peasant (red)	15.00 – 20.00
4th, Scratching head (red)	15.00 – 17.50
5th, Man in pink pants	17.50 – 20.00
6th, Plaid shirt and blue pants	17.50 – 20.00
7th, Colonial man (red)	17.50 – 20.00
8th, Man w/hand to lips	10.00 – 12.00

Second Row:

1st, Green pants, yellow shirt and blue hat, 5" sharp dresser (red)	10.00 – 12.50
2nd, White w/brownish finish (original 10 cent tag on bottom)	10.00 – 12.50
3rd, 7th, 8th and 10th, Men (red)	6.00 – 8.00 ea.
4th, Colonial man (blue)	6.00 – 8.00
5th and 6th, Men	10.00 – 12.50 ea.
9th, Colonial	5.00 – 6.00

Third Row:

1st, Flute player, 5" (red)	8.00 – 10.00
2nd, 7th and 8th, Men	7.50 – 10.00 ea.
3rd, 4th and 6th, Men (red)	6.00 – 8.00 ea.
5th, Man in yellow coat	5.00 – 6.00
9th, Seated man	4.00 – 5.00
10th, White w/brown (red)	7.50 – 10.00

Fourth Row:

1st and 5th, Colonial men, 4"	6.00 – 8.00 ea.
2nd and 3rd, Musketeer and colonial (red)	5.00 – 6.00 ea.
4th, 7th and 8th, Colonial men	2.50 – 4.00 ea.
6th, Man w/hat under arm	5.00 – 6.00
9th, Fiddler (red)	7.50 – 10.00
10th, Guitar player	10.00 – 12.50

Fifth Row:

1st, Man bowing, 6" (green)	20.00 – 22.50
2nd, Man w/basket (red)	12.50 – 15.00
3rd and 7th, Colonial men (red)	15.00 – 17.50 ea.
4th and 6th, Musicians (red)	17.50 – 20.00 ea.
5th, Cowboy (red)	15.00 – 17.50
8th, Man w/yellow cape	12.50 – 15.00

FIGURINES – ORIENTALS

Oriental figurines are no more flattering to them than are those representing us. Lots of fans, kimonos, coolie hats and musical instruments are depicted.

Top Row:

1st, Lady w/fan and yellow skirt, 5"	$10.00 – 12.50
2nd and 8th, Seated or standing girls (red)	8.00 – 10.00 ea.
3rd, Dancer, 6¾" (red)	15.00 – 17.50
4th, Black P.J. (red H.P.)	10.00 – 12.50
5th, Fan lady (blue)	15.00 – 17.50
6th, Lady w/goose	15.00 – 17.50
7th, Little guy	7.50 – 10.00

Second Row:

1st and 2nd, Girl w/fan and boy w/blue top, 4"	6.00 – 8.00 ea.
3rd, Smaller version of 2nd (red)	4.00 – 5.00
4th, 5th and 8th, Girl w/fan, man w/flute and boy w/pig (red)	10.00 – 12.50 ea.
6th, Guy (?)	8.00 – 10.00
7th, Folded hands, 5⅞"	15.00 – 17.50

Third Row:

1st, Lady w/fan, 7½"	12.50 – 15.00
2nd and 3rd, Ladies w/fan (red)	12.50 – 15.00 ea.
4th, Gray lady w/fan, 8"	15.00 – 17.50
5th and 6th, Couple, 8¼"	40.00 – 50.00 pr.
7th, Dancer, 8" (original 29 cents on bottom) (red)	20.00 – 22.50
8th, Mandolin player	10.00 – 12.50

Fourth Row:

1st and 2nd, Same figurine but different painting, 7" (red)	12.50 – 15.00 ea.
3rd, Lady w/basket on head, 7⅞" (red)	20.00 – 25.00
4th, Man w/hands in sleeves (red)	20.00 – 22.50
5th and 6th, Matching bases and marks	17.50 – 20.00 ea.
7th, Similar to 1st and 2nd	12.50 – 15.00
8th, Warrior (red)	12.50 – 15.00

FIGURINES – ORIENTAL (Cont.)

Most of the Orientals found here are pairs or sets. Note the first two girls which are similar. Although the second figure is larger, the first is more detailed and of better quality. Larger is usually better — but not always!

Top Row:

1st, Pink hatted girl w/baskets, 5⅛" (red)	$15.00 – 17.50
2nd, Similar to 1st, 6" (red)	12.50 – 15.00
3rd and 4th, Boys holding hats (red but first has cross hair mark)	12.50 – 15.00 ea.

Second Row:

1st and 2nd, Couple w/boy playing a mandolin, 5½" (red)	25.00 – 30.00 pr.
3rd and 4th, Wall plaques (red "Yamaka")	35.00 – 45.00 pr.
5th and 7th, Violin and tambourine players (red)	8.00 – 10.00 ea.
6th, Mandolin player (red "Yamaka")	8.00 – 10.00

Third Row:

1st – 8th, 4", All priced	8.00 – 10.00 ea.
1st and 6th, (red)	
2nd and 4th, (black)	
3rd, 5th and 8th, Girls all marked (red **E.L.**)	

Fourth Row:

1st, Fan girl, 4⅝"	7.50 – 10.00
2nd – 6th, All bisque ranging from 4" to 4⅝"	10.00 – 12.50 ea.

Fifth Row:

1st, Same as 1st in row above except 4⅛" and (red)	6.00 – 8.00
2nd – 9th, All 4⅛" marked (red). Holding in order: kite, parrot, kite, fly swatter (?), basket, violin, lantern and fan.	7.50 – 10.00 ea.

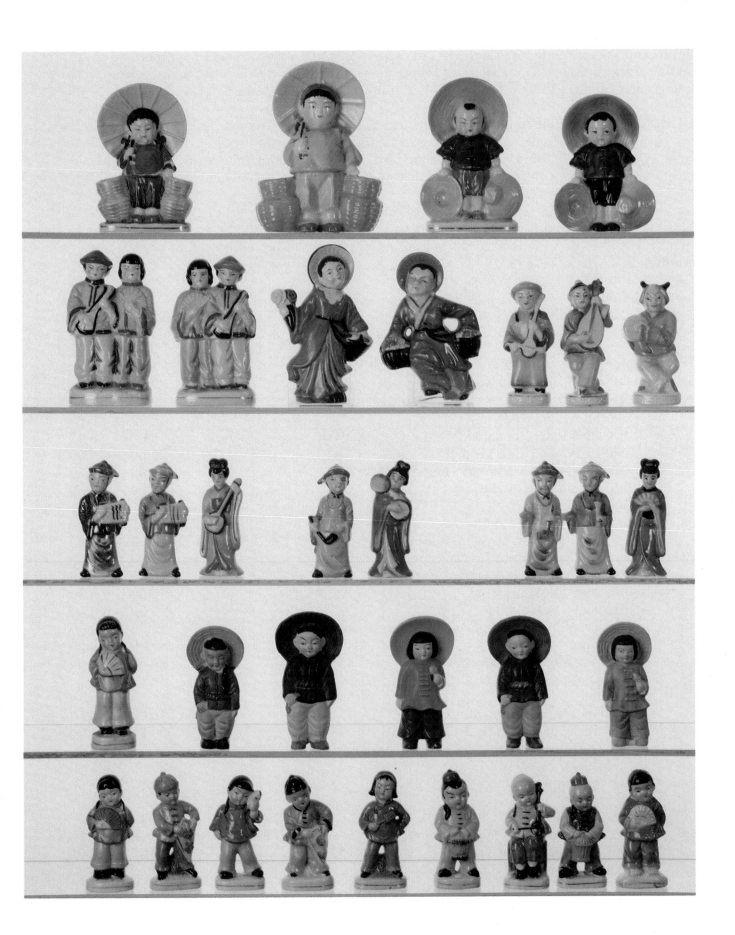

HEAD VASES and MISCELLANEOUS

Prices for Occupied Japan head vases have risen dramatically the last couple of years! The collecting of head vases has become quite a fad. Thus Occupied Japan heads have become even more popular since there are so many more collectors searching for heads. Just this weekend at an collector's extravaganza I saw a booth that had hundreds of these items displayed.

The wooden ship bookends in the top row are quite unusual. Wooden Occupied Japan items are scarce, but these bookends are not very practical since they might hold up only a few paperback books as long as they were small. On the third row are a beautiful creamer and sugar set. The swan handles are very delicate and reminiscent of some of the better known European china makers.

The tiles on the bottom row are embossed on the back. Two are shown so you can see both sides. The bird tile shown in the fourth row is marked in green and not embossed as are the ones on the bottom.

Top Row:

1st – 3rd, Chinese busts (blue)	$22.50 – 25.00 ea.
4th and 5th, Wooden ship bookends (embossed)	65.00 – 75.00 pr.

Second Row:

1st, Girl head vase (green)	22.50 – 25.00
2nd, Lady vase	22.50 – 25.00
3rd, Lady bust (red)	17.50 – 20.00
4th, Bird in tree bud vase (red)	6.00 – 8.00
5th, Lady head vase (orange)	22.50 – 25.00
6th, Boy head vase (green) match to 1st (?)	20.00 – 22.50
7th, Oriental girl vase	15.00 – 17.50

Third Row:

1st, Oriental man jar w/lid (blue)	22.50 – 25.00
2nd and 3rd, Women heads (blue)	15.00 – 17.50
4th, Mandolin player (red)	5.00 – 6.00
5th, Angel w/drum (red)	5.00 – 6.00
6th, Angel w/accordion	5.00 – 6.00
7th, Swan handled sugar w/lid (blue)	45.00 – 50.00
Lid only	20.00 – 22.50
8th, Swan handled creamer (blue)	25.00 – 30.00

Fourth Row:

1st, Sea shell planter (blue)	10.00 – 12.50
2nd, Bird tile (green circle T)	30.00 – 35.00
3rd, Cornucopia (orange "Lamore China entirely hand made G.Z.L. U.S.A.")	30.00 – 35.00
4th – 6th, Card holders (red)	15.00 – 17.50 ea.

Fifth Row:

1st, Small boy with missing top (orange)	5.00 – 6.00
2nd, Floral ring box (red)	12.50 – 15.00
3rd, "Wedgwood" style ring box	17.50 – 20.00
4th and 5th, White tiles (embossed)	12.50 – 15.00 ea.
6th, Heart shaped ring box (orange)	12.50 – 15.00
7th, Hexagonal box w/embossed flower (red)	10.00 – 12.50

LAMPS

Most Occupied Japan lamps are found in pairs. Normally these pairs are mirror images of each other. Note the first pair in the top row and in the second row. Although both of these were bought as pairs, there are some subtle differences in color not normally found on pairs. There are darker colors on the lamp on the right in the top row and more gold on the first lamp in the second row. Most collectors would not take note of color variations, but some collectors are purists who want pairs to match exactly. Forty years later it is hard to argue about small details such as these — but some people will do all possible to buy at a lower price!

Top Row:

1st and 2nd, Courting couple, 6½" (red)	$50.00 – 60.00 pr.
3rd, Basket carrier, 8⅛" (red)	30.00 – 35.00
4th, Cowboy, 7⅜" (red, marked twice)	30.00 – 35.00

Second Row:

1st and 2nd White w/gold Colonials, 7⅜" (red)	55.00 – 65.00 pr.
3rd, Oriental reading book (red)	30.00 – 35.00

Third Row:

1st, Pink hatted lady, 8⅛" (blue)	30.00 – 35.00
2nd, Seated bisque couple "Maruyama"	65.00 – 75.00
3rd, Lady lifting skirt	30.00 – 35.00

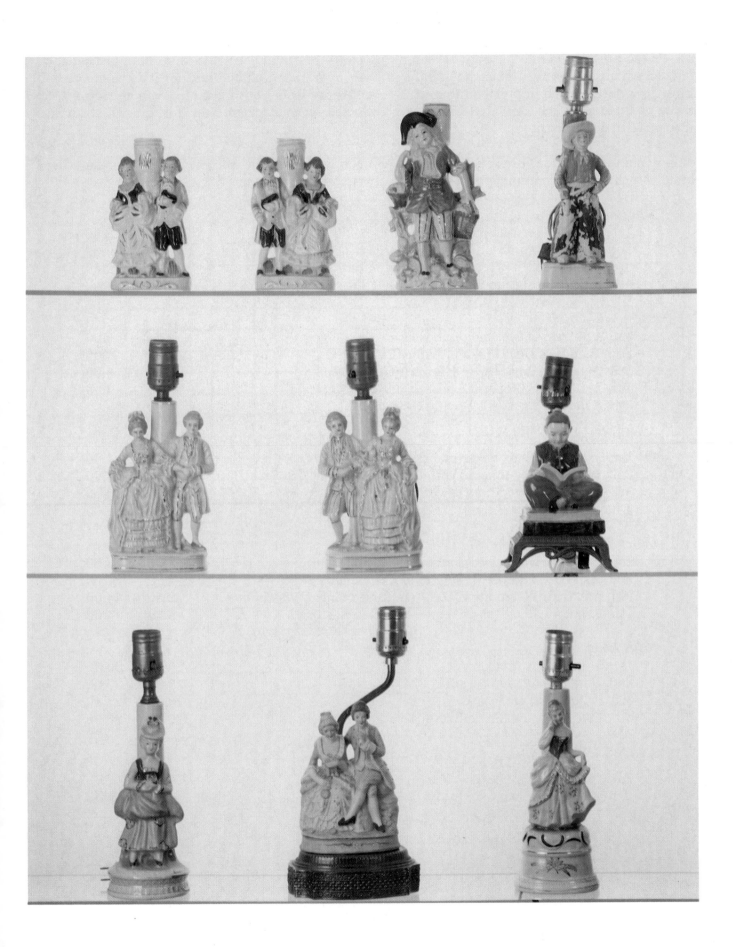

METAL ASH TRAYS and CIGARETTE BOXES

There are still few collectors of metallic Occupied Japan items especially in the smoking accessory line. Prices are reasonable for now, so beginning collectors might want to take note of that fact. Most collectors search for items that relate to their own geographic situation. It is easier to sell Kentucky related items in my shop than it is to sell those from South Dakota. Souvenirs from the Statue of Liberty or the Brooklyn Bridge are collected by more than New Yorkers which makes these more in demand there.

I might point out that the red box with silver decorations in the bottom row is marked silver plated, which is not a common occurrence with Occupied Japan items.

Top Row:

1st, New York crumb pan (embossed)	$10.00 – 12.50
2nd, Ornate Swan crumb pan (embossed)	17.50 – 20.00
3rd, Floral crumb pan (embossed **TK** in diamond)	10.00 – 12.50
4th, Small floral crumb pan (embossed **TK** in diamond)	5.00 – 6.00

Second Row:

1st, Ash tray, St. Joseph (embossed)	2.50 – 4.00
2nd, Ash tray, Birmingham (embossed)	2.50 – 4.00
3rd, Ash tray, Boys Town "Enco, Style No. 21387"	6.00 – 8.00
4th, Ash tray, Sailboat (embossed **SNK** in diamond)	2.50 – 4.00
5th, Ash tray, Football (Prevue Products Inc.)	5.00 – 6.00

Third Row:

1st, Ash tray, Pikes Peak (embossed)	2.50 – 4.00
2nd, Ash tray, Wisconsin Dells (embossed Enco 2T866)	2.50 – 4.00
3rd, Ash tray, New York City (embossed Enco 2T388)	10.00 – 12.50
4th, Ash tray, Washington D.C. (embossed Enco 2T388)	2.50 – 4.00

Fourth Row:

1st, Ash tray, Hollywood (embossed Enco 2T388)	2.50 – 4.00
2nd, Ash tray, Hannibal, Mo. (embossed Enco 2T388)	2.50 – 4.00
3rd, Ash tray, Washington D.C. (embossed Enco 2T388)	2.50 – 4.00
4th, Ash tray, Long Beach (embossed Enco 2T388)	2.50 – 4.00

Fifth Row:

1st, Buddha box (embossed)	25.00 – 30.00
2nd, Pagoda box (embossed)	25.00 – 30.00
3rd, Cupid box (embossed)	20.00 – 25.00
4th, Red box w/sterling silver decoration (embossed)	20.00 – 25.00

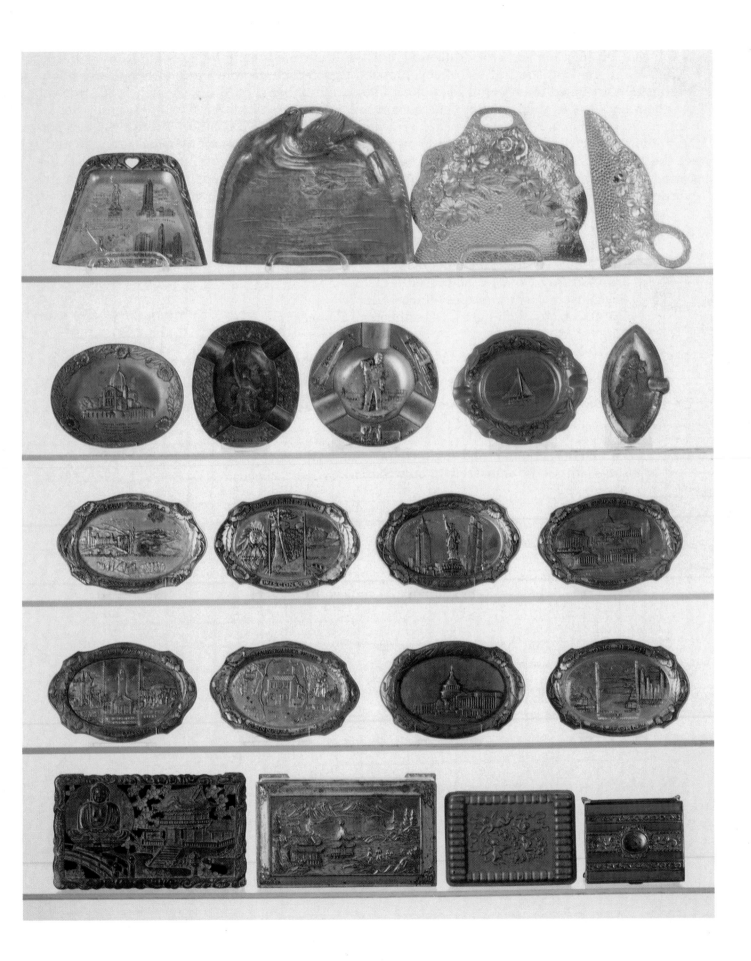

METAL ASH TRAYS, CIGARETTE URNS and MISCELLANEOUS

As you can see smoking accessories abound, but the other metallic items are significantly harder to find. I am showing the full set of seven gods of good fortune this time, although my photographic help arranged them out of sequence. (They are numbered on the base of each.) So you can sort them out, on the shelf reading left to right are No. 7 – Fukurokuju, No. 2 – Jurojin, No. 1 – Benten, No. 4 – Ebisu, No. 6 – Hotei, No. 3 – Daikoku and No. 5 – Bishamon. After a week of photographing Occupied Japan items and using all our scheduled photography time, my wife and I left the metallic and dinnerware items to be photographed at a later date. Believe me unpacking, sorting, measuring, recording data and repacking several thousand items for five solid days gets **extremely** tedious!

Top Row:

1st, Ash tray, Alaska (embossed)	$10.00 – 12.50
2nd, Ash tray, Colorado (embossed)	2.50 – 4.00
3rd, Ash tray, Chicago (embossed)	2.50 – 4.00
4th, Ash tray, leaf w/grapes (embossed)	2.50 – 4.00
5th, Ash tray, Washington, DC (embossed Pioneer)	10.00 – 12.50

Second Row:

1st, 3rd – 6th, Cigarette urns (embossed)	5.00 – 6.00 ea.
2nd, Creamer, (embossed)	7.50 – 10.00
7th, Hand ash tray (embossed)	10.00 – 12.50

Third Row:

1st and 9th, creamer and sugar (rising sun embossed)	15.00 – 17.50 pr.
2nd – 8th, Gods (embossed and numbered)	12.50 – 15.00 ea.

Fourth Row:

1st, San Francisco trolley (embossed)	20.00 – 22.50
2nd, Small sugar (embossed)	8.00 – 10.00
3rd and 4th, Cigarette urns (embossed)	5.00 – 6.00 ea.
5th, Creamer (embossed)	10.00 – 12.50
6th – 8th, Saki glasses or small urns (embossed)	6.00 – 8.00 ea.

Fifth Row:

1st, Pegasus embossed box (embossed)	15.00 – 17.50
2nd, Crown embossed box (embossed)	12.50 – 15.00
3rd, Silent butler (embossed)	20.00 – 22.50
4th, Horse ash tray (embossed)	15.00 – 17.50
5th, Pegasus embossed box (embossed)	15.00 – 17.50

METAL CIGARETTE LIGHTERS and BOXES

Guns were popular lighters as you can see by the eleven different ones shown here. Many of these are still in working order; they still spark when you flick the sparking mechanism.

My experiences in selling lighters have shown that the guns are the fastest sellers and the mother-of-pearl finish is the most desired style of handle.

Top Row:

1st, Gun lighter w/pearl handles (impressed)	$15.00 – 17.50
2nd, Gun lighter on tripod (impressed on grip)	12.50 – 15.00
3rd, Small gun lighter (impressed on trigger guard)	7.50 – 10.00
4th, Large gun lighter on base (impressed on base)	17.50 – 20.00
5th, Small pearl handle lighter (impressed)	8.00 – 10.00
6th, Pearl handle lighter on base (impressed on base)	12.50 – 15.00
7th, Gun lighter on base (impressed on gun end)	8.00 – 10.00

Second Row:

1st, Baby table lighter in box 69¢ sticker MIOJ #20286	5.00 – 6.00
2nd, Hand lighter (C.M.C. silver plate embossed)	12.50 – 15.00
3rd, Champagne bucket lighter (Patricia embossed)	15.00 – 17.50
4th, Urn lighter (crown embossed)	8.00 – 10.00
5th, Pin lighter w/jewels and pearls w/15" chain extension (impressed)	15.00 – 20.00
6th, Gun lighter (imprint on base)	6.00 – 8.00
7th, Gun lighter with base (imprint on base)	8.00 – 10.00
8th, Gun lighter (impressed on trigger guard)	10.00 – 12.50
9th, Pearl handle gun lighter (imprinted base of handle)	10.00 – 12.50

Third Row:

1st, Bottle lighter (impressed side of case)	6.00 – 8.00
2nd and 3rd, Genie lamps (embossed)	12.50 – 15.00 ea.
4th, Basket of fruit (embossed)	10.00 – 12.50
5th and 6th, Set (MIOJ patent applied for)	25.00 – 30.00 set

Fourth Row:

1st, Heart ring box (embossed)	10.00 – 12.50
2nd, Silent butler, paper label	7.50 – 10.00
3rd, Box (embossed)	8.00 – 10.00
4th, Cornucopia on tray, both (embossed)	15.00 – 17.50 set
5th, Horse head ash tray (embossed)	10.00 – 12.50

Fifth Row:

1st, Large book box (embossed world w/wings)	12.50 – 15.00
2nd, Small book box (embossed world w/wings)	10.00 – 12.50
3rd – 5th, Piano boxes (embossed world w/wings)	15.00 – 20.00 ea.
6th, Piano box (embossed bird emblem)	15.00 – 17.50
7th, Piano box (embossed)	12.50 – 15.00

MISCELLANEOUS

No matter how many categories you decide to use in a book, there are always some items which do not fit any of the those you choose. Sometimes objects are left out of a photograph or there are too many items to fit that page where it belongs. In any case, this is the catch-all page.

Top Row:

1st, Plate stand (**SS** in diamond)	$10.00 – 15.00
2nd, Planter (Hand Painted rainbow mark)	8.00 – 10.00
3rd, Owl planter (embossed)	10.00 – 12.50

Second Row:

1st, Piano (orange Ucagco emblem)	7.50 – 10.00
2nd, Pot belly stove	8.00 – 10.00
3rd and 4th, Small horses (red)	6.00 – 8.00 ea.
5th, Bird on tree	7.50 – 10.00

Third Row:

1st, Cucumber	6.00 – 8.00
2nd, Pea pod	6.00 – 8.00

Fourth Row:

1st, Six piece tool set on original card	50.00 – 60.00
2nd, Army of Occupation medal	40.00 – 50.00
3rd and 4th, Cup racks	5.00 – 6.00 ea.

Fifth Row:

1st, Inflatable rubber rooster (purple ink stamped)	17.50 – 20.00
2nd, Inflatable rubber chicken (black ink stamped)	17.50 – 20.00
3rd and 4th, Fuzzy roosters (paper label)	10.00 – 12.50 ea.

PAPER and PAPIER MACHÉ

Most papier maché items are marked "alcohol proof," so they obviously were made to be used for serving drinks. The coasters always seem to be more worn than the trays; they were used!

The box of flags contained a gross (144) with the box marked "Maple Brand #8173; 12 doz." and each flag has a paper label attached.

Top Row:

1st, Coaster (Isco; alcohol proof)	$ 2.50 – 4.00
2nd, Round serving plate (red; alcohol proof)	7.50 – 10.00
3rd, Rectangular tray (green; alcohol proof)	15.00 – 17.50
4th, Small rectangular tray (red)	7.50 – 10.00
5th, Box of eight coasters (red)	30.00 – 35.00

Second Row:

1st, Box of eight coasters (red)	30.00 – 35.00
2nd and 7th, Paper birds	15.00 – 20.00 ea.
3rd, Coaster (red)	2.50 – 4.00
4th, Red round serving plate (Isco, red; alcohol proof)	7.50 – 10.00
5th, Small rectangular tray (red)	7.50 – 10.00
6th, Souvenir plate H.P. "Siloam Springs, Ark."	10.00 – 12.50

Third Row:

1st, Pink barn (blue)	20.00 – 22.50
2nd, Red bowl (silver)	12.50 – 15.00
3rd, American flag (paper)	1.50 – 2.00 ea.
4th, Small rectangular tray (Isco; red)	7.50 – 10.00
5th, Green church (blue)	20.00 – 22.50
6th, Black round serving plate (Isco, red; alcohol proof)	7.50 – 10.00
7th, Blue house (blue)	20.00 – 22.50

PITCHERS and OTHER NOVELTIES

Collectors of miniatures often seek out smaller Occupied Japan objects. The old style print boxes mounted on the wall are used to display these smaller items. You can buy many of these without emptying the checking account and have a quantity displayed without cluttering the whole house.

Top Row:

1st, "Wedgwood" style pitcher w/lady playing mandolin, 2⅝"	$8.00 – 10.00
2nd, "Wedgwood" style pitcher w/lady holding flowers	10.00 – 12.50
3rd, "Wedgwood" style pitcher w/ladies, 4¼"	17.50 – 20.00
4th, Floral pitcher	10.00 – 12.50
5th, Floral pitcher (gold **LD** in face)	12.50 – 15.00
6th, Narrow neck embossed flower pitcher	7.50 – 10.00
7th, Pitcher (red)	5.00 – 6.00

Second Row:

1st, Basket	6.00 – 8.00
2nd, Basket (red "Pico")	5.00 – 6.00
3rd, Blue wicker basket (red "Pico")	6.00 – 8.00
4th, Wishing well	10.00 – 12.50
5th, Basket w/embossed flower	4.00 – 5.00
6th, Lady w/two baskets (hand painted Andrea)	35.00 – 40.00

Third Row:

1st, Wheelbarrow w/roses, 1⅝" x 5"	8.00 – 10.00
2nd, Wheelbarrow w/cherry (hand painted)	6.00 – 8.00
3rd, Wheelbarrow w/yellow flower (red "Pico")	4.00 – 5.00
4th, Blue wheelbarrow (green)	4.00 – 5.00
5th, White wheelbarrow	2.50 – 4.00

Fourth Row:

1st – 3rd, Suitcase, 2" (red)	4.00 – 5.00 ea.
4th, Basket w/grapes (orange)	6.00 – 8.00
5th, Basket w/roses	6.00 – 8.00
6th, Bird handled basket (green)	8.00 – 10.00

Fifth Row:

1st, Blue basket, 2" (red)	3.50 – 5.00
2nd, Open tea pot (red)	2.50 – 4.00
3rd, Coffee w/lid	6.00 – 8.00
4th, Tea pot w/lid	6.00 – 8.00
5th, Blue coffee pot w/lid	6.00 – 8.00
6th, Tea pot w/lid, embossed rose	6.00 – 8.00
7th, Tea pot w/lid (red)	6.00 – 8.00

PLANTER DOGS and MORE DOGS

Many collectors seek out animals, and dogs seem to be one of the favorites to leash. The top two rows and part of the middle are planters or vases. Some of these are strangely colored for dogs, but maybe the color of the planter was more important to the Japanese decorators than the object it depicted. As always, there are stereotyped dogs. Note the fire plug in the third row!

Top Row:

1st, Brown dog, 3⅝" planter	$ 3.00 – 4.00
2nd, Black dog, 4⅝" planter, "rainbow-like" mark	5.00 – 6.00
3rd, Same, orange	5.00 – 6.00
4th, Same, blue	5.00 – 6.00
5th, Same as 1st, black	3.00 – 4.00

Second Row:

1st, Brown dog, 3⅝", sticking out tongue w/top hat planter,	6.00 – 8.00
2nd, Same, black and white	6.00 – 8.00
3rd, Dog planter	17.50 – 20.00
4th, Spotted dog w/basket planter	5.00 – 6.00
5th, Dog w/spotted basket planter	6.00 – 8.00

Third Row:

1st, Dog w/blue ribbon and basket planter	5.00 – 6.00
2nd, Dog w/jaws tied, 1½" (red)	5.00 – 6.00
3rd, Same, only 2⅝"	7.50 – 10.00
4th, Dog w/green basket planter	6.00 – 8.00
5th, Dog resting on sack (red)	6.00 – 8.00
6th, Pair of dogs	6.00 – 8.00
7th, Dog at fire plug	8.00 – 10.00

Fourth Row:

1st, Standing dog (Circle w/**T**)	17.50 – 20.00
2nd, Bird dog (red)	7.50 – 10.00
3rd, Dog holding ball	7.50 – 10.00
4th, Dog holding ball	10.00 – 12.50
5th, Setter (**T** over **M**)	12.50 – 15.00
6th, Bull dog (red)	17.50 – 20.00

Fifth Row:

1st, Begging dog	2.50 – 4.00
2nd, Dog w/blue ribbon	5.00 – 6.00
3rd, Spotted dog	6.00 – 8.00
4th, Bull dog in red hat	12.50 – 15.00
5th, Brown dog (red)	6.00 – 8.00
6th, Group of three dogs (blue)	15.00 – 17.50
7th, Sitting dog	12.50 – 15.00
8th, Dog w/bug on nose	7.50 – 10.00
9th, Poodle w/rose hat (red Ucagco emblem)	17.50 – 20.00

PLANTERS – DONKEYS and OTHERS

Donkey planters seemed to be a favorite of the Japanese for some reason. There are a few zebras and other four legged creatures hauling a cart, but by and large, it is donkeys and more donkeys!

Top Row:

1st, Donkey w/green cart planter	$12.50 – 15.00
2nd, Donkey w/floral cart planter	7.50 – 10.00
3rd, Donkey w/brown cart planter	8.00 – 10.00

Second Row:

1st, Donkey w/cart planter ("rainbow-like" mark)	10.00 – 12.50
2nd, Pack mule planter (brown "rainbow-like" mark)	10.00 – 12.50
3rd, Same as above with different coloring	10.00 – 12.50

Third Row:

1st, Donkey w/cart planter (brown "rainbow-like" mark)	6.00 – 8.00
2nd, Donkey w/cart planter	6.00 – 8.00
3rd, Siesta time w/donkey planter (brown)	12.50 – 15.00

Fourth Row:

1st – 3rd, Donkey pulling cart planters	7.50 – 10.00 ea.

Fifth Row:

1st, Donkey w/two basket planters (brown)	5.00 – 6.00
2nd, Zebra w/basket planter	6.00 – 8.00
3rd, Blue stripped donkey w/two baskets	6.00 – 8.00
4th and 5th, Zebras w/basket	5.00 – 6.00 ea.
6th, Spotted horse (?) w/basket	5.00 – 6.00

PLANTERS – FEATHERED

These might make great Easter floral arrangement holders. At least they are more pleasant to the eye than all the donkey carts.

The third bird in the top row is a creamer, but it seemed to fit here with all the other birds.

Top Row:
      1st, Lady duck in bonnet planter ("rainbow-like mark") $12.50 – 15.00
      2nd, Male duck in top hat planter ("rainbow-like mark")   12.50 – 15.00
      3rd, Chicken pitcher (red)   22.50 – 25.00
      4th, Mallard planter   12.50 – 15.00

Second Row:
      1st, Cygnet planter (hand painted, "rainbow-like mark")   8.00 – 10.00
      2nd, Swan planter (hand painted, "rainbow-like mark")   12.50 – 15.00
      3rd, Swan planter w/wings spread   15.00 – 17.50

Third Row:
      1st, Chickens on planter (red)   5.00 – 6.00
      2nd, Mallard planter   10.00 – 12.50
      3rd, Chicken w/egg planter   15.00 – 17.50
      4th, Chick w/basket planter   5.00 – 6.00

Fourth Row:
      1st, Barnyard goose planter (hand painted)   6.00 – 8.00
      2nd, Rooster pulling egg cart planter   17.50 – 20.00
      3rd, Blue swan (red)   8.00 – 10.00

Fifth Row:
      1st, Green geese planter (blue)   12.50 – 15.00
      2nd, Goose and goslings planter (red)   15.00 – 17.50
      3rd, Duckling w/basket planter   6.00 – 8.00
      4th, Flamingo w/basket planter (brown)   10.00 – 12.50

PLANTERS – PEOPLE

No one can ever accuse the Japanese of slighting florists. There are enough flower containers made in Occupied Japan to supply the needs of florists for years to come.

Top Row:
1st, Oriental girl w/shell planter, 6⅛" (red)	$22.50 – 25.00
2nd, Tulip gal planter (red)	8.00 – 10.00
3rd, Large hatted girl planter	12.50 – 15.00
4th, Rickshaw boy planter (red)	15.00 – 17.50

Second Row:
1st, Accordion player w/dog planter, 4⅛" (red)	10.00 – 12.50
2nd, Lady planter (red)	5.00 – 6.00
3rd, Girl w/dried floral arrangement (red)	6.00 – 8.00
4th, Dutch couple planter	8.00 – 10.00
5th, Girl w/dog planter	8.00 – 10.00
6th, Couple on bench planter	7.50 – 10.00
7th, Child playing violin on fence planter	8.00 – 10.00

Third Row:
1st, Girl w/mandolin planter, 3⅝" (brown)	7.50 – 10.00
2nd, Girl w/horse cart planter	5.00 – 6.00
3rd, Girl w/basket planter (red)	7.50 – 10.00
4th, Duck chasing girl at wall planter	10.00 – 12.50
5th, Dutch guy planter	10.00 – 12.50
6th, Matching Dutch girl planter	10.00 – 12.50

Fourth Row:
1st and 2nd, Girl w/shell planter, 2¾"	5.00 – 6.00 ea.
3rd, Oriental boy w/basket (red)	5.00 – 6.00
4th, Boy on fence (blue)	7.50 – 10.00
5th, Colonial w/basket (red)	5.00 – 6.00
6th, Mexican planter (red)	5.00 – 6.00
7th, Napping musician	6.00 – 8.00

Fifth Row:
1st, Boy w/cherry tree, 3⅝"	7.50 – 10.00
2nd, Shepherd planter	7.50 – 10.00
3rd, Boy w/bird planter (blue)	6.00 – 8.00
4th, Boy w/ fiddle (blue)	7.50 – 10.00
5th, Umbrella boy (hand painted)	8.00 – 10.00
6th, Red hooded lady planter, 4⅝"	8.00 – 10.00

PLANTERS – PEOPLE (Cont.)

Top Row:

1st, Oriental girl w/fan planter, 6⅛" (red)	$10.00 – 12.50
2nd, Man with vase (red)	5.00 – 6.00
3rd, Man with bucket planters, 6¾"	20.00 – 22.50
4th, Girl musician planter (hand painted orange)	7.50 – 10.00
5th, Oriental man matching 1st girl (red)	10.00 – 12.50

Second Row:

1st, Boy skier planter, 3⅜"	7.50 – 10.00
2nd, Girl w/book (hand painted)	7.50 – 10.00
3rd, Girl on bench (red "Pico")	8.00 – 10.00
4th, Boy planter	7.50 – 10.00
5th, Oriental boy w/basket	8.00 – 10.00
6th, Matching girl to 5th	8.00 – 10.00

Third Row:

1st and 2nd, Boy and girl w/cart, 2⅝"	5.00 – 6.00 ea.
3rd and 4th, Boy and girl at well (hand painted)	5.00 – 6.00 ea.
5th, Two children w/wheeled cart planter	6.00 – 8.00
6th, Boy w/horn planter (red)	7.50 – 10.00

Fourth Row:

1st, Boy w/rickshaw planter (hand painted)	10.00 – 12.50
2nd, Oriental girl w/fan planter (red)	12.50 – 15.00
3rd, Girl w/dog planter, 4⅝" (red LD in face)	12.50 – 15.00
4th, Boy musician planter	8.00 – 10.00
5th, Dutch boy planter (brown)	10.00 – 12.50
6th, Boy w/cart planter	12.50 – 15.00

Fifth Row:

1st, Musician w/dog planter, 4⅛" (red)	10.00 – 12.50
2nd, Man walking donkey cart planter (red)	6.00 – 8.00
3rd, Boy w/lamb planter, 5" (green)	12.50 – 15.00
4th, Girl w/goose planter	5.00 – 6.00
5th, Girl w/basket (red)	5.00 – 6.00
6th, Oriental w/large hat planter (red)	7.50 – 10.00

PLANTERS, TOOTHPICKS or SMALL VASES

I have had several readers write that many of the small vases I have shown in the past were actually toothpicks, especially the style of the sixth through the eighth in the bottom row. I have found those with pin cushion holders also. Name them as you wish!

The first dog in the top row looks as if he has been sewn right up the middle; so it was probably designed from a cloth toy of the type popular at that time.

Top Row:

1st, Sewn dog planter, 5¾" ("rainbow-like" mark)	$10.00 – 12.50
2nd, Dogs with doghouse planter (red)	20.00 – 22.50
3rd, Dog pencil holder	7.50 – 10.00
4th, Dog vase (orange)	10.00 – 12.50
5th and 6th, Lounging dog planters ("rainbow-like" mark)	5.00 – 7.00 ea.

Second Row:

1st, Dog in barrel planter	5.00 – 6.00
2nd and 3rd, Dog w/tree stump vase	5.00 – 6.00 ea.
4th, Dog w/basket (blue)	6.00 – 8.00
5th, Dog w/pitcher	6.00 – 8.00
6th and 7th, Dog w/hat or cart	5.00 – 6.00 ea.
8th, Small vase w/bust (red)	7.50 – 10.00
9th and 10th, Vase w/birds in relief (red)	15.00 – 17.50 ea.

Third Row:

1st, Cat watching bird vase (red)	12.50 – 15.00
2nd, Black cat vase (yellow **T** over **M**)	10.00 – 12.50
3rd, Black cat vase (brown **T** over **M**)	10.00 – 12.50
4th, Cat w/vase (brown **T** over **M**)	8.00 – 10.00
5th, Donkey w/cart	2.50 – 4.00
6th, Deer w/basket	4.00 – 5.00
7th, Swan planter	5.00 – 6.00

Fourth Row:

1st and 2nd, Owl on branch (red)	10.00 – 12.50 ea.
3rd and 4th, Chicks vase (red)	5.00 – 6.00 ea.
5th, Ducks vase (red)	6.00 – 7.00
6th, Squirrel watching rooster (brown)	12.50 – 15.00
7th, Squirrel vase (red)	7.50 – 10.00
8th, Bird w/hat vase (red)	6.00 – 8.00

Fifth Row:

1st – 4th, "Wedgwood" style vases, 2¾"	7.50 – 10.00 ea.
5th, "Wedgwood" style vase w/lady and Cupids (orange)	10.00 – 12.50
6th – 8th, Colonial dressed people vases	5.00 – 6.00 ea.
9th and 10th, Martha and George Washington vases, 3¼", (red)	15.00 – 17.50 ea.

SALT and PEPPER SHAKERS

Salt and pepper shakers are gathered by many collectors other than those seeking Occupied Japan shakers. I have seen collectors of Occupied Japan ignore high priced unusual shakers only to see them bought by a shaker collector who did not care that they were marked MIOJ or not.

There are many single shakers shown this time since I bought a collection that had many unmatched pairs. I have found very few mates for these, but it's fun to search!

Top Row:
1st, Clown crouching on drum (circle **T**)	$30.00 – 35.00
2nd, Clown on back on drum (circle **T**)	30.00 – 35.00
3rd and 4th, Cat pair	15.00 – 17.50
5th and 6th, Hat pair (only brown marked)	12.50 – 15.00 pr.

Second Row:
1st, Six piece colonial scene set consisting of jar w/lid and spoon on tray w/salt and pepper	25.00 – 30.00 set
2nd and 3rd, Dutch couple (red)	12.50 – 15.00 pr.
4th, Three piece flowers on basket (basket only marked)	15.00 – 20.00

Third Row:
1st and 2nd, Totem pole set	10.00 – 12.50 pr.
3rd and 4th, Mugs (Watkins Glen, N.Y.)	12.50 – 15.00 pr.
5th and 6th, Pigs (red)	12.50 – 15.00 pr.
7th and 8th, Squirrels	12.50 – 15.00 pr.

Fourth Row: (All singles, so double price for pair)
1st, Toadstool	6.00 – 7.50
2nd, Mexican lady (red)	6.00 – 7.50
3rd, "Hummel-like" boy (red)	6.00 – 7.50
4th, Dutch girl (red)	6.00 – 7.50
5th, Boy w/lederhosen (red)	5.00 – 6.00
6th, Geisha w/fan (red)	7.50 – 10.00
7th, "Hummel-like" boy, 4⅜"	7.50 – 10.00
8th, Bird (Quebec, Canada)	5.00 – 6.00
9th, Dutch boy bust (red)	6.00 – 7.50

Fifth Row:
1st, Toby winker	10.00 – 12.50
2nd, Popeye	17.50 – 20.00
3rd, Duck	6.00 – 7.50
4th, Dutch girl (red)	6.00 – 7.50
5th, Cowboy	7.50 – 10.00
6th, Strawberry	5.00 – 6.00
7th, Seated Dutch girl	6.00 – 8.00
8th, Paddling Indian	6.00 – 7.50

SETS – BEES, COTTAGES and TOMATOES

No matter how many items I find in one of these sets, there always seem to be yet undiscovered pieces lurking someplace! I had not realized how many bee collectors there were until we were deluged with orders for "bee" items in my last book. The honeycomb design seems to attract people nearly as well as bees. Note the beehive variations of size and design in the picture. The lighter colored, green handled pieces are more abundant. There are more people searching to complete these sets.

Cottage sets are found more often in the rectangular shapes. This set with round cottages is harder to collect especially with pieces coming in at least two sizes.

Tomato collectors abound, but Occupied Japan tomatoes are difficult to harvest. I have had several letters and photographs from "tomato" collectors who have large sets, but few of their pieces are marked Occupied Japan. I have not seen many of the unusual tomato pieces in those photographs marked MIOJ, so you might not find demitasse or saki tomato sets marked.

Top Row:
1st, Honeycomb design creamer, 2⅝" (blue)	$10.00 – 12.50
2nd, Sugar w/lid to match (blue)	17.50 – 20.00
3rd, Beehive tea pot w/honeycomb design (**T** in circle)	35.00 – 40.00
4th, Beehive honey jar (Ucagco emblem)	22.50 – 25.00
5th, Bee two part relish (**T** in circle)	17.50 – -20.00

Second Row:
1st, Honeycomb creamer, 2¾"	12.50 – 15.00
2nd – 4th, Three piece set: pepper, mustard, salt (red **K** in circle)	20.00 – 22.50 set
5th, Marmalade hive, (**T** in circle)	15.00 – 17.50
6th, Honeycomb design sugar w/lid	20.00 – 22.50
7th, Honeycomb design honey jar	17.50 – 20.00
8th, Salt and pepper w/green handled holder (only tray marked MIOJ)	15.00 – 17.50 set

Third Row:
1st, Cottage creamer, 2⅝"	12.50 – 15.00
2nd, Cottage creamer, 2" (blue Ucagco emblem)	10.00 – 12.50
3rd, Large sugar to match 1st creamer	22.50 – 25.00
4th and 5th, Salt and pepper	17.50 – 20.00 pr.
6th, Sugar to match 2nd creamer (blue Ucagco emblem)	15.00 – 17.50

Fourth Row:
1st, Tomato sugar	15.00 – 17.50
2nd, Tomato cracker or biscuit jar (Maruhonware **K** in circle)	60.00 – 75.00
3rd, Tomato sugar	15.00 – 17.50

TEA POTS and SETS

Some of the more popular and widely known Japanese designs are shown here. The charcoal gray dragon sets are still copied today in gray as well as additional colors. I have even seen orange dragon sets in Occupied Japan. The popularity of this set makes it highly desired in a completed form. Since these designs have been used so long, it is very hard to find single matching pieces with the same markings or shapes. Note the flat bottomed cup shown next to the demitasse pot in the top row. I have not found a saucer with the right cup ring diameter to match the red wreath marking on the cup. Speaking of that pot, I have never ascertained whether this is a chocolate or demitasse pot. It seems to depend upon whom you ask!

Many pieces of this dragon ware have lithopane bottoms. Hold them to the light and you see a geisha girl pictured in the bottom. These bring up to 50% more than the prices listed!

The third tea pot in the second row is still being made today which should explain how popular that embossed wrap around dragon still is. Very few from the Occupation time period are marked MIOJ. I have seen several of these that only say Japan brought back from Japan by returning soldiers.

Those brown glaze tea pots in the bottom row were prolifically produced, but demand today is sadly lacking.

Top Row:
1st, Dragon creamer (red **M** in wreath)	$ 15.00 – 17.50
2nd, Dragon sugar w/lid (red **M** in wreath)	25.00 – 27.50
3rd, Dragon demitasse cup and saucer (red **M** in wreath)	17.50 – 20.00
4th, Flat bottomed cup (red **M** in wreath)	12.50 – 15.00
5th, Dragon demitasse pot (red **M** in wreath)	75.00 – 85.00
Seventeen piece Dragon set as shown (red **M** in wreath)	235.00 – 265.00

Second Row:
1st, Tea pot, blue trimmed floral (red)	30.00 – 35.00
2nd, Tea pot, floral (blue "Trimont China")	45.00 – 50.00
3rd, Embossed dragon tea pot (blue **KS** in shield emblem)	100.00 – 125.00
4th, Dragon tea pot (red "Shofu China")	75.00 – 85.00

Third Row:
1st and 5th, Floral demitasse cup and saucer (red Ucagco emblem)	12.50 – 15.00 set
2nd, Floral creamer (red Ucagco emblem)	15.00 – 17.50
3rd, Demitasse pot (red Ucagco emblem)	65.00 – 75.00
4th, Floral sugar w/lid (red Ucagco emblem)	22.50 – 27.50
Seventeen piece set as shown (red Ucagco emblem)	190.00 – 215.00

Fifth Row:
1st, Brown tea pot w/embossed flowers	30.00 – 35.00
2nd, Brown individual tea pot (yellow **M** in circle)	20.00 – 22.50
3rd, Blue stoneware tea pot w/bamboo handle (**K** in circle)	25.00 – 30.00
4th, Brown tea pot w/embossed flowers	35.00 – 40.00

TEA POTS and SETS (Cont.)

The cups matching the tea set in the top row are shown stacked in the second row.

I have been unable to find cup and saucer sets to match the pieces in the third row; so if you have any extra, let me know!

The saki set in the bottom row was a popular item for soldiers to bring back to the States. Most of these sets have lithopane saki cups. A geisha girl can be seen in the bottom of the cup when it's held to light, and in some cases, this girl is topless! You wonder why so many were brought back? Only the saki bottle here is marked MIOJ.

Top Row:

1st and 5th, Plate, "Noritake"	$10.00 –	12.50 ea.
2nd, Creamer, "Noritake"	17.50 –	20.00
3rd, Tea pot, "Noritake"	50.00 –	55.00
4th, Sugar w/lid, "Noritake"	25.00 –	27.50

Second Row:

1st and 3rd, Cup and saucer to match 1st row, "Noritake"	12.50 –	15.00 ea.
2nd, Floral tea pot (red)	30.00 –	35.00

Third Row:

1st, Sugar w/lid (gold "Ucagco China" emblem)	30.00 –	35.00
2nd, Tea pot w/lid (gold "Ucagco China" emblem)	75.00 –	85.00
3rd, Creamer (gold "Ucagco China" emblem)	20.00 –	25.00

Fourth Row:

1st, Brown two cup tea pot	15.00 –	17.50
2nd – 8th, Rust dragon saki set (red 372399 on bottle only)	85.00 –	100.00
Saki cup w/lithopane geisha girl	8.00 –	10.00 ea.
Saki bottle only	35.00 –	40.00
9th, Brown tea pot	12.50 –	15.00

TOBIES and STEINS

Collectors of tobies abound from miniature collectors to those who started with English toby mugs from which these are copied. No matter which ones you find, they mostly seem to have a sinister look of that stereotype pirate of days of yore. Miniature collectors gather the ones measuring in the 2" range. Most of these look like small pitchers.

The last stein in the third row is written in German. ("Auf der Alm. Im Wald steht ein Bäumchen das grünt s'ganze Jahr.") I only took Latin, so I'll let someone else translate for me.

Top Row:

1st, Toby pitcher, barkeep holding two mugs, 4⅞" (red)	$30.00 – 35.00
2nd, Stein, three musketeers partying	22.50 – 25.00
3rd, Stein, same scene as 2nd but brown rim	22.50 – 25.00
4th, Winker, pitcher	17.50 – 20.00

Second Row:

1st, Toby w/mustache (hand painted)	30.00 – 32.50
2nd, Individual tea pot, 3⅝" (blue)	35.00 – 37.50
3rd, Toby pitcher, 4⅞"	40.00 – 50.00

Third Row:

1st, Stein, man and woman w/dog, 8½"	35.00 – 40.00
2nd, Mug w/coach scene	12.50 – 15.00
3rd, Stein (see last paragraph above)	35.00 – 40.00

Fourth Row:

1st, Mug w/fishermen	12.50 – 15.00
2nd, Pitcher, 3"	15.00 – 17.50
3rd, Pitcher, 2" (red)	12.50 – 15.00
4th, Pitcher (blue **E.W.**)	20.00 – 22.50
5th, Pitcher (blue **E.W.**)	20.00 – 22.50

TOYS

I have had numerous collectors of toys compliment me on the fairly accurate pricing of the toys in my *Collector's Encyclopedia of Occupied Japan, 4th Series*, but a couple of collectors of Occupied Japan were upset at the "high" prices. At least, I have learned in my twenty years of writing that you cannot please everyone. Be that as it may, all prices in this book are prices I have on the items as they are put in my shop for sale.

Mechanical toys with boxes are more valuable than those without boxes. Condition of the box is not as detrimental to the price as not having a box. Of course many toys did not come with a box. Add $5.00 – $10.00 to the price below for boxed toys.

Top Row:
    1st, "Clever Bear" H5/135 (paper label) $ 45.00 – 55.00
    2nd and 3rd, "Walking Bear" MIOJ on box (paper label)   40.00 – 50.00 ea.

Second Row:
    1st, "Roll over Cat" (**T** over **M**, MIOJ on box) impressed mark in
        metal base   40.00 – 50.00
    2nd, "Playful Cat" ("Tahara" on globe mark, MIOJ on box)
        impressed mark in metal base   25.00 – 35.00
    3rd – 5th, Walking bears (all have paper label MIOJ)   40.00 – 50.00

Third Row:
    1st, "X Car," lady driver ("Showa" made in Tokyo) impressed
        mark in metal base   90.00 – 100.00
    2nd, "Walking Goat," Japan design on box, paper label MIOJ
        on goat   45.00 – 55.00
    3rd, "Baby Tortoise," MIOJ on box, impressed mark on metal
        leg   40.00 – 50.00

Fourth Row:
    1st, "Circus Elephant" (**T** over **M**, Modern Toys, MIOJ on box)
        impressed mark on both feet   95.00 – 110.00
    2nd, "Elephant on Barrel" (MIOJ on box) impressed mark
        on barrel   300.00 – 350.00

Fifth Row:
    1st, "Dancing Couple" (**T** over **M**, Modern Toys, Tokyo
        Pat #1196, MIOJ embossed on guy's back)   40.00 – 50.00
    2nd, Smaller dancing couple, MIOJ embossed on guy's back   30.00 – 40.00
    3rd, "Jumping Dog" (MIOJ on box, paper label on dog)   20.00 – 25.00

TOYS and DOLLS

Dolls are another Occupied Japan item that have avid competition from other collecting fraternities. Doll collectors have been accustomed to purchasing highly priced items for their collections and many have told me that Occupied Japan collectors have a tendency to undervalue these. Celluloid, bisque, composition and black dolls are the types most often sought from our field.

Top Row:

1st, Horn (impressed mark on base)	$ 25.00 –	30.00
2nd, Alligator clickers (card marked, but alligators only Japan	40.00 –	45.00 doz.
3rd, Composition doll, stamped on foot	30.00 –	35.00
4th, Silver haired doll, stamped on foot	22.50 –	25.00
5th, Microscope (box stamped and paper label MIOJ on microscope)	75.00 –	85.00
6th, Beetle clicker in front of box (impressed MIOJ)	5.00 –	6.00

Second Row:

1st, Dionne Quints (stamped on box)	75.00 –	85.00
2nd, Celluloid monkey car mirror hanger	22.50 –	25.00
3rd, Celluloid monkey car mirror hanger	12.50 –	15.00
4th, Box of eight bisque dolls (stamped # 2998, MIOJ on box)	100.00 –	125.00

Third Row:

1st and 2nd, Cameras (embossed)	10.00 –	12.50 ea.
3rd, Mouse (impressed MIOJ # 266)	7.50 –	10.00
4th, Rabbit, hanging (paper label)	7.50 –	10.00
5th, Harmonica ("Butterfly" trade mark, soloist, MIOJ in metal)	15.00 –	17.50
6th and 7th, Harmonicas, "Bright" and "Butterfly" (marked box and impressed in metal)	15.00 –	17.50 ea.
8th and 9th, Compasses (impressed mark on edge or back)	17.50 –	20.00 ea.

Fourth Row:

1st, "Special Police" badge (MIOJ on card)	12.50 –	15.00
2nd, Piano baby (hand painted "Andrea")	65.00 –	75.00
3rd, "Meyi Grand" on top and stamped MIOJ on bottom	65.00 –	75.00
4th, Mirror (blue on side)	7.50 –	10.00
5th, Pistol (impressed on side)	12.50 –	15.00
6th, Ukulele (stamped on front below fret)	40.00 –	50.00
7th, Water pistol, bird embossed on side (MIOJ impressed with SR in diamond)	6.00 –	8.00

Fifth Row:

1st, Badminton shuttlecock (stamped below rubber top)	8.00 –	10.00
2nd, Doll in basket (stamped)	30.00 –	35.00
3rd, Black doll impressed mark	45.00 –	50.00
4th, Pair black dolls in box stamped in blue #7521	60.00 –	75.00
5th, Baby stamped mark	30.00 –	35.00
6th, Ping pong ball, tube marked MIOJ "Sonsco"	12.50 –	15.00
7th, Small composition doll (stamped and embossed)	22.50 –	25.00
8th, Snow baby w/seal	35.00 –	40.00

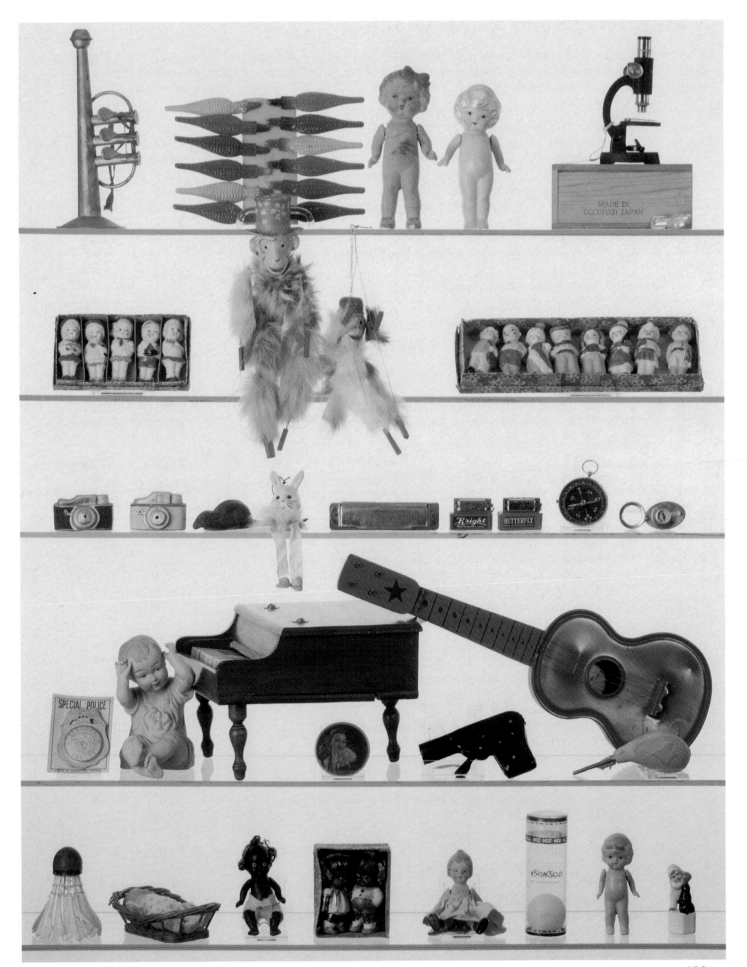

VASES, VASES and MORE VASES

The vases on this page range in height from 1¾" to 6¼". If you are looking for a small vase, then Occupied Japan can fill your every need or want no matter what shape or color you wish. This is only a small, representative sample of what is available!

Top Row:

1st, Vase, 3¾", embossed yellow rose (red)	$17.50 – 20.00
2nd, Vase, 3⅜", blue floral (red "Meiko China," **MK** in wreath)	17.50 – 20.00
3rd, Vase, 5⅞", blue w/gold handles	22.50 – 25.00
4th, Vase, pink w/embossed blue rose (red)	20.00 – 22.50
5th, Vase, 6", urn style (red)	20.00 – 22.50
6th, Vase, 6¼", urn style (hand painted, red)	22.50 – 25.00
7th, Vase, white blossoms (red)	12.50 – 15.00
8th, Vase, green with floral scene (red)	8.00 – 10.00
9th, Vase, yellow and blue striped (blue "Meiko China," **MK** in wreath)	12.50 – 15.00
10th, Vase, green w/embossed red rose (red)	25.00 – 30.00

Second Row:

1st and 2nd, Vases, 4¼", green w/embossed rose	15.00 – 17.50 ea.
3rd, 4th and 8th, Vases, green, blue or white w/embossed flowers (red)	7.50 – 10.00 ea.
5th and 6th, Vases, yellow w/embossed flowers (red "Maruyama")	10.00 – 12.50 ea.
7th, Vase, rose w/lace (red)	15.00 – 17.50
9th, Vase, pink w/white roses (blue)	7.50 – 10.00
10th – 13th, Vases, orange or white w/flowers	4.00 – 5.00 ea.

Third Row:

1st and 2nd, Vases, "Wedgwood-like" w/pink rose	7.50 – 10.00 ea.
3rd, Vase, 1¾", pink, fluted top	5.00 – 6.00
4th and 11th, Vases, 2", white	2.50 – 4.00 ea.
5th, Vase, 1⅞", gold handles	2.00 – 3.00
6th, Vase, pink w/embossed flower (red)	5.00 – 6.00
7th, Vase, brown w/roses	4.00 – 5.00
8th, Vase, 3½" ("Meiko China," **MK** in wreath)	12.50 – 15.00
9th and 10th, Vases, orange w/embossed flowers	7.50 – 10.00 ea.
12th, Vase, green w/white spots (red)	8.00 – 10.00
13th and 14th, Vases, 3⅝", white w/pink flower (red)	10.00 – 12.50 ea.

Fourth Row:

1st, 9th and 10th, Vases, 4¼" (red)	12.50 – 15.00 ea.
2nd, Vase, 4¼" (red "Pico")	12.50 – 15.00
3rd and 5th, Vases, white floral (red)	5.00 – 6.00 ea.
4th, Vase (red)	2.00 – 3.00
6th, Vase, two handled floral	4.00 – 5.00
7th, Vase, pear shaped (hand painted "Pico")	12.50 – 15.00
8th, Vase, garden scene (red, hand painted)	10.00 – 12.50
11th, Vase, Iris (brown **LD** in face emblem)	10.00 – 12.50

Fifth Row:

1st, Vase, 3½", orange flower (brown **LD** in face emblem)	10.00 – 12.50
2nd, Vase, 3⅝", berries (red)	10.00 – 12.50
3rd, Vase, pink corn (**K** in circle)	15.00 – 17.50
4th, Vase, floral (red)	10.00 – 12.50
5th Vase, blue w/red tulip (red hand painted "Pico")	10.00 – 12.50
6th, Vase, cornucopia (red)	10.00 – 12.50
7th, Vase, pagoda scene	15.00 – 17.50
8th and 9th, Vases, embossed dragons (red)	15.00 – 17.50 ea.
10th, Vase, green w/flowers (red)	7.50 – 10.00
11th, Vase, carriage scene	6.00 – 8.00

UNUSUAL and LARGE

Figurines over 10" marked Occupied Japan are hard to find in pairs. For some reason, one figurine in pairs that size is usually damaged or missing. I have sold many figurines over 10" in height, but very few pairs!

The 11¼" bisque clock with angels is a real favorite! Although several people have tried to talk my wife, Cathy, out of it over the last few years, none have succeeded so far. It sits on a shelf in the window of my shop to entice all the Occupied Japan collectors who visit Grannie Bear!

Top Row:

1st, Colonial lady w/fan, 12"	$ 75.00 – 85.00
2nd, Bisque clock w/angels, 11¼" (**AA** "Ardalt Lenwile China," hand painted, #6291 Pat. USA, Model W, AC 110 V, 60 cycle, 2.5 watt)	500.00 – 550.00
3rd, Colonial man to match 1st lady, 12"	75.00 – 85.00
1st and 3rd pair	175.00 – 200.00

Second Row:

1st, Vase, 11¼", scenic view (gold elephant head **A**)	90.00 – 100.00
2nd, Oriental dancer, 14¼" (blue **R** in shield)	100.00 – 125.00
3rd, Lady w/sideways collar, 10⅛"	50.00 – 60.00

UNUSUAL and LARGE (Cont.)

Shown on the opposite page are a wool hooked rug and a phonograph that was sent to me several years ago by George D. Smith to photograph for my book. Somehow the photograph was misplaced at my publishers and is just now being used! I will list the instructions verbatim that George sent years ago. It did take a while to figure it out even with these explicit instructions. This was quite a portable record player for those days of 78's.

1) Place machine on table with Mikky phone sign up.
2) Push silver button on right side.
3) In left cover remove speaker – fits tight.
4) Remove hand crank at base of machine on right side.
5) Turn three-fingered dial to clear on side and tighten down center screw.
6) Remove Mickey (sic) phone by pulling up.
7) On right side push up to the top of the machine, a 180° turn the folded metal arm.
8) Open the three fingers, to the stops.
9) Take the metal speaker, place so opening is down and attach needle part. Has semi-lock on it.
10) Raise small arm up and slide speaker onto it.
11) Crank goes into side and turn it. Please do not wind tight.
12) Place record on the 3-fingers.
13) Pull needle arm down 90° until it is over the button that you used to open the machine.
14) Record is now turning. Place needle on record.
15) Should be all set.

Top photograph:
    Mikky phonograph 4½" x 5¾" long x 4" tall (metal tag on box) $150.00 – 200.00
Bottom photograph:
    Wool hooked rug 3' by 5' (cloth MIOJ tag)   75.00 – 100.00

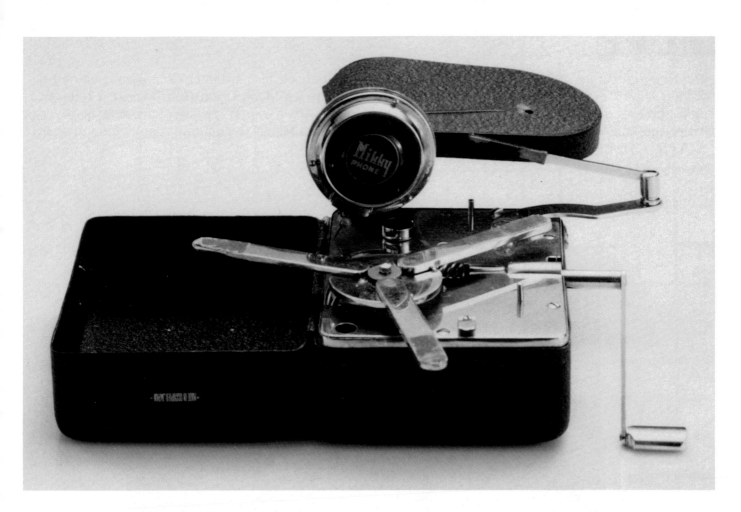

UNUSUAL

At an outdoor flea market near Pittsburgh, I found this book last summer. The owner valued it higher than I did, but since I had never owned a **book printed in Occupied Japan**, I relented and purchased it. The book is 7⅛" x 5" and titled "Floral Art of Japan". Shown here are the cover, title page and copyright page showing it to be printed in 1949 in Occupied Japan. Value of book $65.00 − 75.00

Arranged by Mrs. Riei Ikeda

This novel, though artistic group is an example of the sanjūike (triple arrangement)

FLORAL ART OF JAPAN

BY
ISSŌTEI NISHIKAWA

JAPAN TRAVEL BUREAU

EDITORIAL NOTE

To satisfy the desire of tourists on flying trips to Japan to learn something of the art, culture and customs of the country, the Board of Tourist Industry in 1934 began publishing the Tourist Library Series, designed to comprise a set of over a hundred brochures, each dealing with a different phase of Japanese life and culture.

After the completion of forty volumes, the Board in 1934 transferred all publishing rights to the Japan Travel Bureau, which is endeavoring to carry on with same high purpose of its predecessor.

The volumes of the first series now being out of print and the demand for more copies increasing daily in insistence, we have begun a new series,——revising and reprinting some of the old volumes, and issuing others on entirely new and equally interesting subjects. Each volume is the work of a recognized authority on the subject, and is profusely illustrated with excellent photographs and illustrations.

It is hoped that by perusing these brief but comprehensive studies of the various phases of Japanese life the reader will gain some insight into the unique culture that has developed in this country throughout the ages.

Japan Travel Bureau

UNUSUAL (Cont.)

Shown at the bottom of this page are a pair of Occupied Japan figurines obviously copied from designs used by "Florence Ceramics" of California. In December of 1988 I interviewed Florence Ward, the founder and maker of "Florence Ceramics" at her home in Anaheim, California. She still has a disdain for Japanese copy-cat artists because they caused her to go out of business. Although she successfully sued them for copyright infringement of her figurines, they continued to copy her work without another problem by changing a position of an arm, head or some other minor difference which fell outside the copyright laws. Due to the immense popularity of Florence ceramic figures today, it's entirely possible the prices on these MIOJ copies will escalate over the next few years.

On the next page are Japanese "flies." At the top is a fly swatter and the bottom is a boxed fly rod. The label on the box says "Beautiful fine quality, the best available in Japan" in the red strip at the top. Inside the red fish it says "Akai Trademark" and on the blue strip "Akai Fishing Goods Co., Ltd" in white ink. The MIOJ mark is also printed on the blue strip in black. The white strip says "Split Bamboo Fishing Pole." This four-section pole box originally held flies and fishing line. My Dad has a similar boxed set made after the occupation that has all the original pieces included in the box. I bought this set out of Washington and it obviously was used for the original purpose.

> *Bottom page 118:*
> 1st, Boy, 9", "Florence" look-a-like ("Maruyama") $35.00 – 40.00
> 2nd, Girl mate, 8¼", same marks   35.00 – 40.00
>
> *Page 119:*
> 1st, Fly swatter   22.50 – 25.00
> 2nd, Fly rod in box (box marked)   50.00 – 60.00

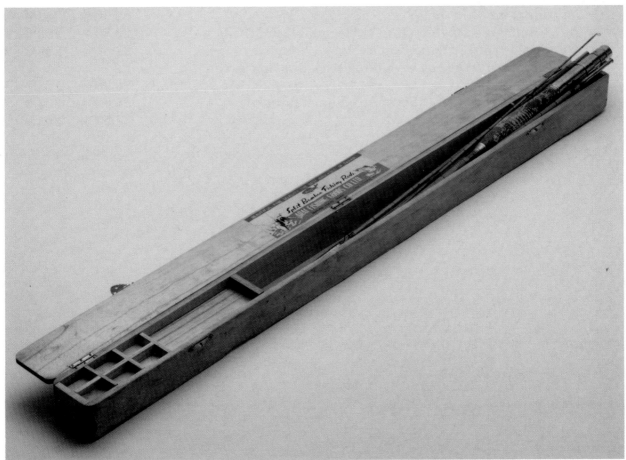

LATE ARRIVALS

It never fails that when you finish photographing for a book, the next day or even on your way home from the photography session a sensational or unusual piece "attacks" you wanting to be included in the book. Such was the case this time, and since that session was a year ago, there were several pieces found that are shown in the next two photographs. There were more, but space limitations prevail at this point in order to print economically.

Top Row:

1st, Coach, 6" x 9" (red "Maruyama")	$150.00 –	200.00
2nd, Man holding flowers, 10½"	65.00 –	75.00
3rd, Seated lady w/book, 6" (red "Maruyama", SAMPLE)	40.00 –	45.00

Second Row:

1st, Seated lady w/golden lace holding rose (red **T** over **S**)	80.00 –	90.00
2nd, Standing lady w/golden lace holding rose (red **T** over **S**)	100.00 –	115.00
3rd, Standing w/golden lace (red **T** over **S**)	80.00 –	90.00
4th, Standing lady w/crinoline puffed skirt (red **T** over **S**)	50.00 –	60.00
5th, Mate to 4th (red **T** over **S**)	50.00 –	60.00

Third Row:

1st, Cupid holding shell	27.50 –	30.00
2nd, Cupid blowing horn on footed box (gold "Ucagco China" emblem)	65.00 –	75.00
3rd, Angel w/rose heart shaped crinoline topped box (red)	35.00 –	40.00
4th and 5th, Babies riding butterfly (red)	17.50 –	20.00 ea.

Fourth Row:

1st, Cupid type kid (blue)	22.50 –	25.00
2nd, Cupid type kid (blue **R** in circle and black MIOJ)	22.50 –	25.00
3rd, Cupid type kid (blue **R** in circle)	22.50 –	25.00
4th, "Hummel" type boy w/walking stick and dog (green)		
5th, Oriental boy	10.00 –	12.50
6th, Black boy w/dice – "Seven" (red hand painted)	25.00 –	30.00
7th, Girl w/dog (red)	17.50 –	20.00

LATE ARRIVALS (Cont.)

One of the more unusual items is found in the third row on the right side. The barber has a place to drop in old razor blades. It was neat enough I had to buy it when I first saw it.

Top Row:

1st, Cow creamer (blue)	$35.00 – 40.00
2nd, Parrot planter	35.00 – 40.00
3rd, Bird planter (blue)	15.00 – 17.50
4th, Nude handled mug (red)	25.00 – 30.00

Second Row:

1st and 2nd, Martha and George salt and pepper shakers (red #02020)	17.50 – 20.00 pr.
3rd, Cat and bird cage on tree shakers (tree MIOJ, but shakers red Japan)	15.00 – 17.50 set
4th, Oriental carrying basket shakers (blue)	22.50 – 25.00 set
5th, Flowering cabbage shakers on stand (blue **R** in heart shaped design)	15.00 – 17.50 set

Third Row:

1st, "Walking Small Bear" (paper sticker on bear; **T** over **M**, Modern Toys on box)	40.00 – 50.00
2nd and 3rd, Cats (red **S** in semicircle)	
4th, Parrot car swinger (OJ on suction cup; embossed on red stick)	7.50 – 10.00
5th – 7th, Birds (OJ on suction cup; embossed on red stick)	6.00 – 8.00 ea.
8th, Barber "Blades" disposal in head	40.00 – 50.00

Fourth Row:

1st, Cigarette box w/horse scene (blue)	15.00 – 17.50
2nd, Ash tray for above box	2.50 – 4.00 ea.
3rd, Metal lighter (imprinted mark)	12.50 – 15.00
4th, Small lighter (imprinted mark)	6.00 – 8.00
5th, Mouse (imprinted mark)	7.50 – 10.00
6th, Rose embossed bowl and cover (red)	25.00 – 30.00

COVER DESCRIPTION

Most of the pieces shown on the cover are photographed elsewhere in this book, but a couple of the pieces were shown in my *Collector's Encyclopedia of Occupied Japan, 4th Series*. Cover photographs were made for both books at the same time, and it was hard to visualize which pieces would be in each book a year ahead of the time I would write them.

Left foreground:
    Couple at piano, 5½" (gold **L.D.** in flower face emblem) $ 50.00 – 65.00
    Bisque piano baby (hand painted "Andrea")   50.00 – 65.00

Left background:
    Bisque clock w/angels, 11¼" (**AA** "Ardalt Lenwile China," hand
        painted, #6291 Pat. USA, Model W, AC 110 V, 60 cycle,
        2.5 watt)   500.00 – 550.00

Center foreground:
    Lacquerware basket w/metal handle ("Maruni")   55.00 – 65.00

Center background:
    Oriental dancer, 14¼" (blue **R** in shield)   100.00 – 125.00

Right foreground:
    Lady w/children on embossed floral shoe, 5" high (gold
        "Chikusa")   65.00 – 75.00

Right background:
    Horse w/rider, 10¼" (hand painted "Andrea")   150.00 – 175.00

Other Books By Gene Florence

Collectible Glassware from the 40's, 50's & 60's $19.95

Collector's Encyclopedia of Akro Agate Glassware,
  Revised Edition $14.95

Collector's Encyclopedia of Depression Glass, 11th Edition $19.95

Collector's Encyclopedia of Occupied Japan I $14.95

Collector's Encyclopedia of Occupied Japan II $14.95

Collector's Encyclopedia of Occupied Japan III $14.95

Collector's Encyclopedia of Occupied Japan IV $14.95

Elegant Glassware of the Depression Era, 5th Edition $19.95

Florence's Standard Baseball Card Price Guide, 6th Edition $9.95

Kitchen Glassware of the Depression Years, 4th Edition $19.95

Pocket Guide to Depression Glass, 8th Edition $9.95

Very Rare Glassware of the Depression Years $24.95

Very Rare Glassware of the Depression Years, Second Series $24.95

Very Rare Glassware of the Depression Years, Third Series $24.95

Books on Antiques and Collectibles

This is only a partial listing of the books on antiques that are available from Collector Books. All books are well illustrated and contain current values. Most of the following books are available from your local book seller, antique dealer, or public library. If you are unable to locate certain titles in your area, you may order by mail from COLLECTOR BOOKS, P.O. Box 3009, Paducah, KY 42002-3009. Customers with Visa or MasterCard may phone in orders from 8:00 – 4:00 CST, M – F – Toll Free 1-800-626-5420. Add $2.00 for postage for the first book ordered and $0.30 for each additional book. Include item number, title, and price when ordering. Allow 14 to 21 days for delivery.

BOOKS ON GLASS AND POTTERY

10	American Art Glass, Shuman	$29.95
16	Bedroom & Bathroom Glassware of the Depression Years	$19.95
12	Blue & White Stoneware, McNerney	$9.95
59	Blue Willow, 2nd Ed., Gaston	$14.95
19	Coll. Glassware from the 40's, 50's, 60's, 2nd Ed., Florence	$19.95
11	Collecting Yellow Ware – Id. & Value Gd., McAllister	$16.95
52	Collector's Ency. of Akro Agate Glassware, Florence	$14.95
73	Collector's Ency. of American Dinnerware, Cunningham	$24.95
72	Collector's Ency. of California Pottery, Chipman	$24.95
12	Collector's Ency. of Children's Dishes, Whitmyer	$19.95
33	Collector's Ency. of Cookie Jars, Roerig	$24.95
24	Collector's Ency. of Depression Glass, 11th Ed., Florence	$19.95
09	Collector's Ency. of Fiesta, 7th Ed., Huxford	$19.95
39	Collector's Ency. of Flow Blue China, Gaston	$19.95
15	Collector's Ency. of Hall China, 2nd Ed., Whitmyer	$19.95
34	Collector's Ency. of Majolica Pottery, Katz-Marks	$19.95
58	Collector's Ency. of McCoy Pottery, Huxford	$19.95
13	Collector's Ency. of Niloak, Gifford	$19.95
39	Collector's Ency. of Nippon Porcelain I, Van Patten	$19.95
89	Collector's Ency. of Nippon Porcelain II, Van Patten	$24.95
65	Collector's Ency. of Nippon Porcelain III, Van Patten	$24.95
47	Collector's Ency. of Noritake, 1st Series, Van Patten	$19.95
34	Collector's Ency. of Roseville Pottery, Huxford	$19.95
35	Collector's Ency. of Roseville Pottery, 2nd Ed., Huxford	$19.95
14	Collector's Ency. of Van Briggle Art Pottery, Sasicki	$24.95
33	Collector's Guide To Harker Pottery - U.S.A., Colbert	$17.95
39	Collector's Guide to Shawnee Pottery, Vanderbilt	$19.95
25	Cookie Jars, Westfall	$9.95
40	Cookie Jars, Book II, Westfall	$19.95
75	Czechoslovakian Glass & Collectibles, Barta	$16.95
15	Elegant Glassware of the Depression Era, 5th Ed., Florence	$19.95
18	Glass Animals of the Depression Era, Garmon & Spencer	$19.95
24	Kitchen Glassware of the Depression Years, 4th Ed., Florence	$19.95
22	Pocket Guide to Depression Glass, 8th Ed., Florence	$9.95
70	Red Wing Collectibles, DePasquale	$9.95
40	Red Wing Stoneware, DePasquale	$9.95
58	So. Potteries Blue Ridge Dinnerware, 3rd Ed., Newbound	$14.95
39	Standard Carnival Glass, 4th Ed., Edwards	$24.95
48	Very Rare Glassware of the Depression Years, Florence	$24.95
40	Very Rare Glassware of the Depression Years, Second Series	$24.95
26	Very Rare Glassware of the Depression Years, Third Series	$24.95
27	Watt Pottery – Identification & Value Guide, Morris	$19.95
24	World of Salt Shakers, 2nd Ed., Lechner	$24.95

BOOKS ON DOLLS & TOYS

79	Barbie Fashion, Vol. 1, 1959-1967, Eames	$24.95
10	Black Dolls - 1820 - 1991 - Id. & Value Guide, Perkins	$17.95
14	Character Toys & Collectibles, 1st Series, Longest	$19.95
50	Character Toys & Collectibles, 2nd Series, Longest	$19.95
29	Collector's Ency. of Barbie Dolls, DeWein	$19.95
38	Collector's Ency. of Disneyana, Longest & Stern	$24.95
41	Madame Alexander Price Guide #18, Smith	$9.95
40	Modern Toys, 1930 - 1980, Baker	$19.95
42	Patricia Smith's Doll Values – Antique to Modern, 9th ed	$12.95
86	Stern's Guide to Disney	$14.95

2139	Stern's Guide to Disney, 2nd Series	$14.95
1513	Teddy Bears & Steiff Animals, Mandel	$9.95
1817	Teddy Bears & Steiff Animals, 2nd Series, Mandel	$19.95
2084	Teddy Bears, Annalees & Steiff Animals, 3rd Series, Mandel	$19.95
2028	Toys, Antique & Collectible, Longest	$14.95
1808	Wonder of Barbie, Manos	$9.95
1430	World of Barbie Dolls, Manos	$9.95

OTHER COLLECTIBLES

1457	American Oak Furniture, McNerney	$9.95
2269	Antique Brass & Copper, Gaston	$16.95
2333	Antique & Collectible Marbles, 3rd Ed., Grist	$9.95
1712	Antique & Collectible Thimbles, Mathis	$19.95
1748	Antique Purses, Holiner	$19.95
1868	Antique Tools, Our American Heritage, McNerney	$9.95
1426	Arrowheads & Projectile Points, Hothem	$7.95
1278	Art Nouveau & Art Deco Jewelry, Baker	$9.95
1714	Black Collectibles, Gibbs	$19.95
1128	Bottle Pricing Guide, 3rd Ed., Cleveland	$7.95
1752	Christmas Ornaments, Johnston	$19.95
2132	Collector's Ency. of American Furniture, Vol. I, Swedberg	$24.95
2271	Collector's Ency. of American Furniture, Vol. II, Swedberg	$24.95
2018	Collector's Ency. of Granite Ware, Greguire	$24.95
3430	Coll. Ency. of Granite Ware, Book 2, Greguire	$24.95
2083	Collector's Ency. of Russel Wright Designs, Kerr	$19.95
2337	Collector's Guide to Decoys, Book II, Huxford	$16.95
2340	Collector's Guide to Easter Collectibles, Burnett	$16.95
1441	Collector's Guide to Post Cards, Wood	$9.95
2276	Decoys, Kangas	$24.95
1629	Doorstops – Id. & Values, Bertoia	$9.95
1716	Fifty Years of Fashion Jewelry, Baker	$19.95
3316	Flea Market Trader, 8th Ed., Huxford	$9.95
3317	Florence's Standard Baseball Card Price Gd., 5th Ed.	$9.95
1755	Furniture of the Depression Era, Swedberg	$19.95
3436	Grist's Big Book of Marbles, Everett Grist	$19.95
2278	Grist's Machine Made & Contemporary Marbles	$9.95
1424	Hatpins & Hatpin Holders, Baker	$9.95
3319	Huxford's Collectible Advertising – Id. & Value Gd.	$17.95
3439	Huxford's Old Book Value Guide, 5th Ed.	$19.95
1181	100 Years of Collectible Jewelry, Baker	$9.95
2023	Keen Kutter Collectibles, 2nd Ed., Heuring	$14.95
2216	Kitchen Antiques – 1790 - 1940, McNerney	$14.95
3320	Modern Guns – Id. & Val. Gd., 9th Ed., Quertermous	$12.95
1965	Pine Furniture, Our American Heritage, McNerney	$14.95
3321	Ornamental & Figural Nutcrackers, Rittenhouse	$16.95
2026	Railroad Collectibles, 4th Ed., Baker	$14.95
1632	Salt & Pepper Shakers, Guarnaccia	$9.95
1888	Salt & Pepper Shakers II, Guarnaccia	$14.95
2220	Salt & Pepper Shakers III, Guarnaccia	$14.95
3443	Salt & Pepper Shakers IV, Guarnaccia	$18.95
3737	Schroeder's Antiques Price Guide, 12th Ed.	$12.95
2096	Silverplated Flatware, 4th Ed., Hagan	$14.95
3325	Standard Knife Collector's Guide, 2nd Ed., Stewart	$12.95
2348	20th Century Fashionable Plastic Jewelry, Baker	$19.95
3444	Wanted To Buy, 4th Ed.	$9.95

Schroeder's
ANTIQUES
Price Guide

. . . is the #1 best-selling antiques & collectibles value guide on the market today, and here's why . . .

8½ x 11, 608 Pages, $12.95

• *More than 300 advisors, well-known dealers, and top-notch collectors work together with our editors to bring you accurate information regarding pricing and identification.*

• *More than 45,000 items in almost 500 categories are listed along with hundreds of sharp original photos that illustrate not only the rare and unusual, but the common, popular collectibles as well.*

• *Each large close-up shot shows important details clearly. Every subject is represented with histories and background information, a feature not found in any of our competitors' publications.*

• *Our editors keep abreast of newly-developing trends, often adding several new categories a year as the need arises.*

If it merits the interest of today's collector, you'll find it in *Schroeder's*. And you can feel confident that the information we publish is up to date and accurate. Our advisors thoroughly check each category to spot inconsistencies, listings that may not be entirely reflective of market dealings, and lines too vague to be of merit. Only the best of the lot remains for publication.

Without doubt, you'll find
SCHROEDER'S ANTIQUES PRICE GUIDE
the only one to buy for
reliable information and values.

COLLECTOR BOOKS
A Division of Schroeder Publishing Co., Inc.